Other People's Software Endeavours

Mathias Weber

Other People's Software Endeavours

Texts: © Copyright by Mathias Weber

Cover Design: © Copyright by Mathias Weber

Book Title: Other People's Software Endeavours
Author: Mathias Weber
Published by: Mathias Weber
Publication Date: January 8, 2024
Residence: Berlin, Mitte District
Email: miesauweder80-mathias_weber_berlin@yahoo.com

Mathias Weber

The author kicked off his adventure into the world of business by diving into business administration studies, though he quickly pivoted to business informatics—what he fondly calls the business administration of the 21st century. For the past five years, he's been thriving as an IT consultant. About two years ago, his curiosity took him beyond the confines of his day job and into the buzzing tech scene. He started sharing his insights on LinkedIn and soaking up inspiration at tech events in Berlin. A passionate conversationalist at heart, he turned these events into playgrounds for sharpening his listening skills.

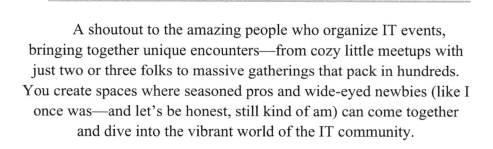

A shoutout to the amazing people who organize IT events, bringing together unique encounters—from cozy little meetups with just two or three folks to massive gatherings that pack in hundreds. You create spaces where seasoned pros and wide-eyed newbies (like I once was—and let's be honest, still kind of am) can come together and dive into the vibrant world of the IT community.

Table of Contents

Prologue

When I stepped into the hotel, a sense of dread already gripped me. The people standing and smoking outside the Mercure Hotel Airport Düsseldorf were French. The fact that I'd had mixed experiences with French people in the past wasn't even the issue; after all, that could be chalked up to the language barrier. No, what made my mind race with anxiety could be summed up in a single word: bedbugs.

Since reports of bedbugs in Paris went viral and sparked a wave of panic, I, a consultant constantly on the move, had one more worry added to my list. After the summer 2023 bedbug scare, France had become, in my mind, the "land of bedbugs." My mental cinema replayed scenes of bedbugs crawling on seats in the Paris Metro nonstop. Instagram, with its addictive Reels, only fueled the anxiety. The logical conclusion I'd reached was that the French must be carrying these tiny pests from their picturesque country to the rest of the world.

Deep down, I knew this fear wasn't rational, but as a human, I am still a creature of emotions. I didn't have the time to research every niche topic that triggered my anxieties until I felt calm again. So, I simply braced myself and pushed forward.

On an uncomfortably muggy Monday evening in mid-September 2023, I checked into the Mercure Hotel Airport Düsseldorf. The hotel was neither in Düsseldorf nor near the airport—I knew that much already. Still, I was in for a surprise. At check-in, the reception staff informed me that this four-star hotel had no air conditioning. If only I had put my professional snobbery aside and booked the Ibis Budget next door, which, as it turns out, did have air conditioning. After the

11

recent heatwave and with temperatures still reaching up to 30 degrees Celsius, this annoyed me.

Then came the next ambush when I entered my room. It looked as though it hadn't been updated since the 1970s. My paranoid eye immediately began scanning the sheets for bedbugs. Unfortunately, I did find something. It wasn't bedbugs, just some ordinary spiders and ticks—or at least that's what I told myself. How would I know the difference anyway? I'm someone who finds botany dreadfully boring, so I wasn't exactly an expert.

To calm myself down, I drew on my "survival skills" from a semester abroad in Siberia, ordered a cheese-stuffed pizza from Domino's, and turned on the TV.

A flash of lightning, followed by a powerful clap of thunder. The ominous clouds looming in the sky had finally decided to unleash their pent-up fury in a thunderstorm. Normally, it would have been a fantastic atmosphere, especially when one was safe in a hotel room. Normally. But then there was the pizza. After a long, hot day on the train and the disappointing check-in, my basic trust in the workings of the universe was a bit shaken. So, I wasn't entirely convinced that the pizza delivery driver would be able to get past the hotel's parking gate. Irrational? Sure, mea culpa.

So, I braved the storm for a Hawaiian pizza with cheese-stuffed crust, waiting by the parking gate for ten minutes. It was pouring rain, with flashes of lightning and terrifying thunder all around. By sheer luck rather than any sound decision-making, I got my pizza, dashed back to my room, and enjoyed every bite while watching an episode of *South Park* on Comedy Central.

Was my life no longer at risk after that? Not quite. The next morning, I got up extra early to make time for reading *The Gulag*

Archipelago in the original Russian and for a morning walk. I loved morning walks, especially before starting work. I was also eager to explore the somewhat desolate area around the hotel. The night before, I'd already mapped out a route to the nearest gas station on Google Maps, where, in an ideal world, I'd pick up a sugar-free Monster Energy drink and let the caffeine, fresh air, and exercise send me into bliss.

But my hopes were short-lived. After five steps out of the hotel, I saw the sky's looming threat above me. Five more minutes down the path, as I walked along a country road, the threat became reality: rain, lightning, and thunder. My umbrella protected me from the rain, but against lightning, it would be useless. Gritting my teeth, I abandoned the walk and turned back to the hotel.

Annoyed as I was, I tried to make the best of the situation. I opened the September issue of my magazine, *iX* (a journal for professional information technology), and continued reading. I hoped that by immersing myself in its articles, I could gain an edge over the competition on my journey to becoming the CTO of a mid-sized German DAX-listed company.

I had read somewhere that chess players who not only practiced the game but also studied chess literature gained a significant advantage over their less studious peers. I love reading, so this approach wasn't a challenge for me.

That said, I would have much preferred to be outside near a gas station, leisurely sipping a Monster Energy drink. Instead, I found myself engrossed in an article about SBOMs.

SBOM stands for *Software Bill of Materials*. These bills of materials are designed to alleviate the constant paranoia of IT security professionals regarding potential vulnerabilities. Often, there is little clarity about what exactly goes into a piece of software. For a long time, much like the production of sausages, people preferred not to know what was in their software—as long as it worked and kept customers happy.

Then came a fateful day in December 2021, when a server for the online video game *Minecraft* was targeted in an attack exploiting a vulnerability in a software component called Log4j. This component is part of many widely used software applications. Unsurprisingly, just seven days after the attack on the gaming server, systems belonging to the Belgian military were also taken offline.

While SBOMs in formats like SPDX (Software Package Data Exchange), CycloneDX, and CPE (Common Platform Enumeration) cannot prevent such attacks, they enable IT departments to quickly assess their exposure when new vulnerabilities are discovered.

In the end, the article went a long way toward restoring my mood, making up for some of the frustration I had felt earlier.

Using FreeNow, an app that lets people like me order and pay for taxis with minimal human interaction, I booked a ride to my client's location. With 20 minutes to spare before the taxi arrived, I decided to have the breakfast I couldn't cancel. I hoped it would be worth the €5.60 that would be deducted from my tax-free meal allowance.

The scrambled eggs were decent. The coffee, however, was dreadful. It was so bad that I couldn't even look the kind, elderly Italian man serving breakfast in the eye. Distressed, I gazed out from my table at the hotel's outdoor area, letting my thoughts drift. Why was I putting myself through all this?

Admittedly, some of the challenges were self-inflicted, rooted in my personality. That said, I did enjoy my exploratory walks around the hotels I was often assigned to visit. Yet I couldn't help but wonder if life could be simpler, more focused on leisure. But that's not who I am. I aim high—not at any cost, mind you, or I'd probably have studied finance and become an investment banker.

Instead, my knack for numbers and analytical thinking led me to switch from business administration (BWL) to a grueling program in business informatics. I loved business administration, but I didn't feel attractive or confident enough for that world. I'd rather be a reserved business informatics graduate in a sea of charismatic BWL alumni.

In that field, I promised myself, no one would care during a job interview whether I was impeccably dressed, came across as charming, or had aced every soft-skill course with top marks. And I was right—finding a job after earning my bachelor's degree was surprisingly straightforward.

But once I entered the workforce, I realized the real game was just beginning.

Chapter 1 - Fog of War

When I arrived in Berlin three years ago in February, I had no idea where to begin. The city felt like it was shrouded in a massive, impenetrable fog. One day in the future, perhaps it will be possible to upload all the essential information about a city directly into one's mind through a neural interface—ideally tailored to the needs of newcomers.

But for now, I was still a prisoner of my limited biological hardware. Google Maps could answer basic questions about the nearest grocery store or döner shop, but that wasn't why I had moved to Berlin. When people asked me why I had come to Berlin, I always gave the same answer: "Berlin's tech scene."

It was perhaps the vaguest response I could have given, yet most people nodded knowingly. "Ah yes, the infamous Berlin tech scene." Berlin, Europe's tech hub. But there was one problem with my answer: I genuinely meant it. It wasn't some excuse to hide the fact that I had come here just to party. Because I hadn't.

There it was—the fog. Or rather, two kinds of fog. The usual, everyday fog and the tech-scene fog. The regular fog, I was confident, would naturally lift over time. Eventually, even my dense, square-shaped head would figure out where the nearest supermarket was, the best route to my office, which döner was worth trying, and which nearby streets to avoid because of the more aggressive types lurking there.

The tech-scene fog, however, was a tougher nut to crack. I felt like I owed something, though I wasn't entirely sure what. One thing was certain: one day, I wanted to puff up my chest like a proud songbird and confidently declare, *"I know Berlin's tech scene as well as I know the menu at Kentucky Fried Chicken in Russia."*

But to get there, I'd first have to clear the tech fog in my head.

I compared Berlin's city map to the map in the video game *Age of Empires*. At the start of the game, parts of the map are shrouded in fog. In the game, the fog obscures areas that haven't yet been explored by the player. In real life, I could see Berlin's map clearly, but I had no way to gauge the strategic importance of individual locations.

For example, was Google's office at Tucholskystraße 2 a key hub in the cosmos of Berlin's tech scene, or was it irrelevant—a mere façade in a Potemkin village constructed by the trillion-dollar corporation? Had it been established simply to distract from where the real action was happening elsewhere?

In *Age of Empires*, the "fog of war" is a key gameplay mechanic, and understanding it is essential. To lift the fog, the player must physically explore the area. This is achieved in the game by sending out scouts.

The fog also holds strategic significance. Before a player can make effective decisions, they must gather information about the terrain, enemy movements, and resource locations. The fog introduces an element of uncertainty, as it conceals the actions of opponents, enabling ambushes and surprise attacks.

Additionally, exploring an area once is not enough. As soon as scouts leave a region, the fog returns, requiring multiple explorations to maintain visibility. During the game, players can develop skills and technologies to expand their field of view or even permanently uncover parts of the map.

Could the lessons from the "fog of war" be applied to my Berlin tech-scene fog? Absolutely—and quite effectively at that. I would take on the role of the scout myself, at least until I had a team of actual scouts working under me. By attending local events, I would gather information—insights about the places where the tech scene thrived, as well as about its current activities and "movements."

Surprises were to be expected, and I needed to prepare myself mentally for them. Perhaps I'd find myself at events where, for reasons unknown, I wasn't particularly welcome. Or I might encounter situations I hadn't anticipated. Visiting or exploring a single event wouldn't suffice, of course. Attending events and lifting the tech fog would need to become an ongoing effort. Without a broad base of experiences, I wouldn't be able to draw accurate conclusions.

Finally, I'd need to develop new skills and adopt emerging technologies to permanently clear parts of the fog. After all, my youthful energy was a finite resource—one that, as it diminished with age, I would need to compensate for by continually upgrading my abilities and tools.

Although the tech fog was present from the very beginning—lingering in my mind alongside the "fog of war" metaphor—and I intuitively understood the importance of attending local events, it still took some time after moving to Berlin before I developed a sustainable strategy.

At first, I sporadically attended tech events I found through the Meetup app. At the same time, I discovered a tool that allowed me to engage with the tech scene more effectively: writing. I began publishing online articles on various tech topics that were relevant to my work as a Data Architect and Data Engineer.

A few events here, a few LinkedIn articles there—it felt like I was heading in the right direction. But I couldn't shake the feeling that I could take it even further.

The decisive breakthrough came to me on October 6, 2022, during an evening event about the proper operation of AI software. As I watched, admittedly full of envy and resentment (mea culpa, I know), one of my cheerful colleagues successfully co-organizing the event, my brain kicked into high gear.

My online articles were cool and visible, but they weren't really scalable. I couldn't exactly write 100 articles about the same topic. On the other hand, attending events was cool and scalable but lacked visibility. I could attend 100 events, but who would ever know?

Another issue also gnawed at me: my memory. I struggled to recall the details of the events I had attended. The further back they were, the fuzzier my recollections became. I couldn't even remember whether I had attended certain events in spring or summer of the same year.

What was the point of attending 100 events if, a few years later, I wouldn't remember any of them?

Synthesis is the merging of two (or more) components into a greater whole. Turning two into one. Online articles on one side, events on the other. Something began to click in my overactive mind. Then, a flash of inspiration struck: why not write online articles about the events I attended?

On the way back, I made a decision: 100 online articles about 100 IT events I would attend.

The battle plan was set. There was only one thing left to say: *"Time's up, let's do this."* Followed by a bold and enthusiastic: *"LEEROY JENKINS!"*.

Chapter 2 - Sluggish Slow-Motion

After a thirty-minute walk home, I felt the exhaustion setting in. It had been a long day. I had spent an hour studying for my Requirements Engineer certification in the morning before work, followed by a productive day collaborating with my friendly Polish colleagues (C# developers who shared my exact sense of humor). On top of that, I'd attended an evening event.

It was time to call it a night. Tomorrow was another day. Besides, I needed to wake up early enough to dedicate an hour to reading *The Idiot* by Fyodor Dostoevsky before heading to work. My first event report could wait until the next evening—or maybe even Saturday morning.

I felt deeply connected to Prince Lev Myshkin, the protagonist of Dostoevsky's *The Idiot*. Like him, I was an idiot. While his story began after a five-year stay in a Swiss sanatorium, mine began after completing a bachelor's degree and a twelve-month internship.

Granted, one can hardly compare time spent in a Swiss sanatorium to attending Saarland University—especially since my university life, marked by grueling exams and an ever-present fear of failure, could hardly be described as a healing experience. Still, one thing is certain: both settings are artificial environments, shielding one from the real world outside.

And so, like the young Prince Myshkin, I began my journey as a socially awkward misfit. Like him, I was initially ridiculed for my naive ideas and behavior. I once heard a YouTuber say, "Nobody takes you seriously until you're 30." That gave me some comfort.

The thought of my first event report occupied my mind all Friday at work. At exactly 5:30 PM, with the weekend finally ahead of me, I opened my personal laptop and logged into LinkedIn. Without delay, I began writing my first event report—still without numbering, as the idea of numbering them hadn't occurred to me yet.

The report came together quickly; after all, I'd spent the entire day eagerly waiting to let my fingers fly across the keyboard of my cheap yet reliable laptop. When I saw the finished report, I felt a deep sense of satisfaction—but also an urge for more.

I couldn't resist, so I immediately wrote four additional event reports. Before that fateful evening at my colleague's exclusive gathering, I had already attended several events. While I couldn't recall all of them, the ones I still remembered were carefully documented.

For the moment, my hunger was satisfied. I went to bed.

The following week, I found an excuse to delay fully committing to my event-reporting odyssey: I had to attend a CDU (Christian Democratic Union) event. I had joined the CDU back in high school and, now that my studies were behind me, I wanted to revive my involvement with the party.

Two weeks after publishing my first five reports, I wrote another one—this time about an event I had attended more than four months earlier. However, I kept losing track of how many reports I had written, so a few months later, I decided to number each one: #1, #2, #3, and so on. The numbering followed the chronology of when the events took place, not when the reports were published.

As a result, my first published event report ended up being #6. Details matter.

As a Data Engineer, my daily work revolved around moving data from point A to point B as elegantly and automatically as possible. Along the way, I had to transform it into a format that made it easy for the target audience at point B to consume. Naturally, I started attending events with a focus on data and data management.

I vaguely recalled a data engineering event hosted by the delivery service Flink, but the memory was too hazy to create an event report from it. The problem was clear: there simply weren't many events centered on data as their main theme. This put me in a bit of a bind. To find enough relevant events, I realized I might need to travel to other cities.

I decided to test this approach and headed to Hamburg. Despite it being a regular workweek, my employer happened to have an office in Hamburg, and the high-speed ICE train made the trip in just two hours. This allowed me to attend an evening event hosted by DAMA, a data management association. From that event came my first chronologically accurate event report.

As I mentioned before, everything that came prior had been swept away by the whirlpool of forgetfulness.

Fortunately, three months later, I found and attended the next data-focused event, this time in Berlin. Unlike the previous one held in an impressive office building overlooking Hamburg's Elbphilharmonie, this event took place in a run-down "Berlin chic" venue called Betahaus. I enjoyed the presentations—they inspired me to do more.

However, I realized that the data theme felt too narrow for me. By this point, I had started to see myself more as a solution architect: someone who elegantly connects various programs and software to solve complex problems. With that perspective, I felt ready to broaden my horizons.

I decided to attend not just events about data processing but also those focused on information processing—in essence, anything IT-related. This way, I wouldn't need to travel to Hamburg or other cities as often. After all, Berlin had no shortage of IT events.

Between June 9, 2022, and November 23, 2022, I attended a total of ten events. Four took place in the Google ecosystem, two in the Microsoft ecosystem, and four were independent in nature. At most of these events, I felt quite comfortable in my role as a solution architect.

However, at my seventh event on October 26, 2022, I felt distinctly out of place—like I wasn't attractive enough for the room. Unwittingly, I had walked into a gathering that was primarily composed of finance professionals. They were all impeccably dressed and blessed with enviable genetics. Ah, the world of finance. I used to admire it. The subject has always captivated me intellectually.

Yet I've never felt that I could truly fit in with the stereotypical "finance type." Most of them seem driven solely by money, and unfortunately, that often attracts some rather unpleasant characters—in other words, jerks.

But I made it through that event unscathed.

My appetite was whetted, the format was established, but the pace was sluggish. I wasn't happy with that at all. In five months, I had only managed to gather material for ten event reports. At that rate, it would take me 50 months to reach my goal of attending 100 events—over four years. Weak.

I knew I had to drastically accelerate my efforts. To do that, I needed to systematize the process and integrate it into my daily routine. From then on, I set myself a goal: to attend at least one event per week and immortalize it in a LinkedIn report.

It was an ambitious challenge. Inspired by the Netflix series *BoJack Horseman*, I told myself: *"It gets easier every week. Every week, it gets a little easier. But you have to do it every week. That's the hard part."*

Chapter 3 - Questionable Vial

Just as I was ready to really pick up speed, the year was already drawing to a close, and everything started shutting down. I couldn't entirely escape the seasonal slowdown. Still, I managed to squeeze in three more events in December (#11–#13) before I, too, succumbed to the general winter pause.

Attending three events in December was a small improvement. At that rate, it would now take me just three years to reach my goal of 100 events. Of course, I consoled myself with the thought that a normal month would have allowed for more progress. That eased my conscience a bit.

On top of that, I wrote a LinkedIn article about access control in the Internet of Things with Amazon Web Services and studied for a Google Cloud certification. So, the month wasn't entirely wasted.

Of the three December events, one stood out in particular: my first DevFest. When spoken aloud, it sounds a bit like "DeathFest"—not the most inviting name. Someone should probably revisit that. Nevertheless, I liked it.

I learned that Google enthusiasts organize local developer festivals every year in many major cities around the globe. I attended the Berlin edition in 2022. Unlike other events, it took place during the day and on a Saturday. That meant, for once, I could show up well-rested and full of energy—a dangerous combination.

Few people share my easily ignited enthusiasm, which quickly turns me into an overbearing companion. But I didn't mind. The excitement was worth it.

On Saturday, December 3, 2022, the first Saturday of December, I set out far too early. Before heading to the event, I wanted to pick up a copy of *All Quiet on the Western Front* from a nearby Amazon Locker. The Netflix film based on the book had left a strong impression on me.

With nearly an hour to spare before the event, I sought refuge from the cold and the falling snow in a nearby café and began reading the book. It was even more intense than the film. Grateful that I wasn't required to contribute my talents to a world war yet, I paused my reading and made my way to the DevFest happening nearby.

The venue transported me to a distant future, a stark contrast to the trenches of World War II depicted in *All Quiet on the Western Front*. The DevFest took place in the rooms of c-base e.V., a (fictional) reconstruction of a crashed space station. The place was genuinely cool and lived up to its description on Wikipedia. It was filled with quirky features and intricately designed details. For members of the organization, there was even a private room in the basement.

The atmosphere, the air, and the regular crowd took me back to my days as a business informatics student, walking past the student common rooms of the computer science department. There, I'd often see my computer science peers enjoying their daily breakfast together. Back then, I struggled with theoretical computer science and never truly felt like part of that intellectual elite—just a "hyphen informatician," caught between business and IT.

At the event, I spotted a familiar face—someone I had seen at other events. To me, he was the epitome of a computer scientist, and I had never dared to approach him. For no good reason, I feared he might expose me as nothing more than a "hyphen informatician," someone dabbling in computer science purely for economic motives.

Ironically, he shared the same first name as I do. Even today, we didn't strike up a conversation.

The DevFest was an undeniable success. I exchanged thoughts and ideas with eight different people, spanning a range of ages and genders. Even I was surprised by my social skills.

I also learned several valuable things: how much CO_2 and electricity can be saved when developing an app, what it takes to become a recognized Google Developer Expert (GDE), and how to effectively analyze spaghetti code.

The event left me with a strong sense that I was heading in the right direction with my odyssey.

Between Christmas and New Year's, I met up with close friends in my hometown. At a Café Extrablatt, I devoured a cheese-drenched cheeseburger while my friends made something painfully clear: as outsiders to my field, they couldn't fully grasp the value of a professional certification. However, they could immediately recognize the absence of a master's degree—a grim revelation for someone like me, without one.

After all, my goal was to reach a level where only outsiders would be hiring me. I decided then and there to pursue a master's degree alongside my job. One less flaw to weigh me down.

The new year began with a bang. Almost as if it were no big deal, I committed to spending approximately €13,000 over the next three years on a part-time master's program. A third of that would be reimbursed through tax deductions, but it was still money I could have put to good use elsewhere.

Even before the first payment went to the distance learning university, I attended my first event of 2023 (#14). Organizing an event as early as January 11th earned my respect for the organizers.

Reaching the AI Campus, the event venue, turned out to be more challenging than expected. Although I was already familiar with the location (from event #7), Google Maps decided to play tricks on me, leading me astray through rainy Berlin. I was on the verge of giving up, convinced I'd be at least 10 minutes late.

But as I reminded myself, not everything would go smoothly when attending 100 events. Determined, I decided to push on. Soaked and exhausted, I arrived just in time for the first talk in the far-too-small room at the AI Campus.

Pleased with my small victory, I listened as the speakers shared their experiences and insights from a computational linguistics conference in Abu Dhabi.

New year, new resolutions, new energy. The very next day, I attended another event (#15). Three compelling reasons motivated me to overcome my fatigue from the day before and take part.

First reason: the building. During previous walks, the building at Zimmerstraße 50 in Berlin had caught my eye several times, almost painfully, due to its beauty. At first, I thought it might be an opera house—but it wasn't.

Second reason: Axel Springer. The Axel Springer Group, or one of its brands, is a household name in Germany. You can't escape it. The new Axel Springer building, along with some of the company's offices, is located at Zimmerstraße 50.

Third reason: Palantir. This very building, at this very company, was hosting the world's first Foundry developer meetup. Foundry is an analytics platform developed and operated by Palantir. From the media, I knew that Palantir counted intelligence agencies like the CIA, FBI, and NSA among its clients. A triple win.

Of course, such a stunning building deserved an equally impressive security checkpoint. I initially couldn't get past it. The scan of my coat revealed a small bottle I wasn't aware of. After some back-and-forth, I finally found the culprit: a bottle of hand sanitizer I'd stashed in my coat during the pandemic.

The rest of the evening went smoothly. At the meetup, I was surprised to discover how similar Foundry was to the analytics platform I worked with daily. You never stop learning.

Chapter 4 - Champagne Party in Monaco

With many colleagues, I can't shake the feeling that they've completely handed over responsibility for their professional development and career advancement to their employer from the moment they started their job. Their mindset seems to be: *"Boss says, I do. Boss doesn't say, I don't do."*

In my opinion, this is a mistake—not because of any malice on the part of their bosses, but because an employer's goals only partially align with those of an employee. Companies primarily seek stability and predictability, and employees' professional development and career paths are subordinated to those priorities.

Additionally, decision-making processes in companies are agonizingly slow. By the time I convince my boss to pay for a certification, a lot of time has already passed. Due to budget constraints, I might only get approval for one certification and the necessary study time every two years.

If I'm willing to invest my own money and time, I can complete five certifications or more in a single year. The competencies I build in this much shorter timeframe can then serve as a strong argument for a promotion or more exciting responsibilities.

It's easy to see why I chose not to involve my employer in my "100 Events" project. Sure, it would have been cool to attend and document events during work hours, but I'm confident my employer would never have allocated the budget for it. The financial cost alone would have been enormous.

A simple calculation makes this clear. As a consultant, my time— every day, even every hour—is billed to clients. While I don't know the exact rate my employer charges clients (and couldn't disclose it for legal reasons even if I did), friends, acquaintances, and internet sources suggest that €800 per day is the absolute minimum for a consultant.

If we estimate the time commitment for one event at a minimum of three hours—two hours to attend (often more) and at least one hour to document it in a report—that's 300 hours for 100 events. Three hundred hours translates to 37.5 eight-hour workdays. At €800 per day, that's €30,000. Even though I consider myself a persuasive speaker, convincing my boss to spend at least €30,000 (and likely much more) on this project feels entirely out of reach.

There's another reason I chose not to involve my employer in this ambitious project: ownership. I wanted full and exclusive control over the project and anything that might result from it. This way, my employer couldn't interfere. For this reason, I've been meticulous about avoiding any mention of my employer. My paranoia even extended to a decision not to attend any of my employer's events, even if they were public.

Despite being a personal initiative, my daily work naturally benefited from the lessons I learned through my project. I casually picked up new concepts and ideas that enriched my role as a solution architect. At event #16, for instance, I learned that not all cloud storage solutions support the new Delta Lake format because their protocols lack optimistic locking when writing data. Alongside other technical details about streaming data, I also became more familiar with the venue at Zimmerstraße 78, which I had first encountered at event #12.

Once again, the presenter was abruptly interrupted at 7:45 PM by the self-cleaning cycle of the coffee machine. With its steaming and hissing, the machine stole the spotlight and, after a brief moment of surprise, had the audience laughing yet again.

Two days later, I experienced the unfortunate spectacle of an event at the AI Campus (#17) that almost entirely lacked any technical depth. It was a fireside chat with a founder who had previously worked at well-known IT startups in Berlin. The format promised an intimate discussion, and the keynote speaker began with a reasonably engaging introduction. However, as her easily digestible monologue progressed, I started to pick up serious "rich kid" vibes.

With each passing sentence, she dug herself deeper into the hole, and her millionaire's child aura became overwhelming. Perhaps my reaction was also influenced by my complete lack of interest in the HR topics that dominated her talk. Frankly, I've always been skeptical of people who are genuinely passionate about HR work.

I couldn't shake the feeling that she and her friends had only become part of Berlin's start-up scene because they'd grown bored of sailing trips to Sylt, skiing in St. Moritz, and polo tournaments in English counties. It didn't seem like they were chasing big money or taking significant personal risks. No, they were just looking for distraction and variety.

Instead of blowing their parents' money on champagne parties in Monaco, they founded start-ups. At least, that was the impression her personal anecdotes—liberally sprinkled throughout her monologue—left on me.

Fortunately, this evening was an exception. After that, no speaker ever gave me a similar vibe again. My adventure could continue, free from the nagging feeling I'd had that night: that I was missing a healthy dose of "Vitamin Trust Fund" to move forward.

I came to understand the consequences of exhaustion at my next event on Wednesday, February 8, 2023 (#18). The day started energetically with a 90-minute study session for my part-time master's degree, continued ambitiously with a full day of work at the office (by choice, since I was allowed to work entirely remotely), and ended with me crashing into the crashed spaceship at c-base.

This time, it was a meetup for PHP developers. While I wasn't particularly familiar with the language, programming concepts are usually transferable to other languages I know better. The speaker, a Frenchman (pre-bedbug panic), seemed determined to make me question my career choices.

His topic, "Lazy Loading of Web Content," initially piqued my interest. However, his heavy French accent during his English presentation and his abstract, professor-like delivery style ultimately drove me to flee. The fact that he'd already done a trial run of this talk at a conference in Disneyland Paris didn't help his case.

Exhausted from my day and worn out by the Frenchman's words, I left the spaceship—which felt like it had just crashed again—and sought refuge at my favorite döner shop. There, I bought myself two dürüms to help me decompress.

The next two events (#19 & #20) more than made up for the previous experience. At event #19, in a pleasant atmosphere, I deepened my DevOps knowledge, connected with a few other developers, and learned how to cleverly hijack the Fishbowl discussion format to promote one's own start-up.

Event #20 continued on a positive note. Developers from the delivery industry presented various technological considerations related to the "last mile"—the final stretch to the customer's doorstep. Although the host kicked off the event by cursing large tech companies, including my employer or its partners, the rest of the event proceeded harmoniously without further discord.

Chapter 5 - Piles of Money

My journey of attending events raised many doubts and questions within me: Would I even find enough worthwhile IT events to attend? Would I be welcome everywhere? How would I handle situations where I wasn't welcome? Would the event content eventually become repetitive, leaving me with nothing new to report? Could I balance the additional workload with my job and my master's program? Would my colleagues laugh at me for this ridiculous project? And, ultimately, would this project turn out to be a complete waste of time? How long would it take me to reach my goal of 100 events?

At least regarding the last question, my optimism was growing. In January and February 2023 alone, I attended 11 events. What had previously taken me over five months, I now managed in just under two. I felt a growing momentum as I looked back on the events I had attended so far. The diversity of topics and groups surprised me, as did my own energy to juggle my master's program and my political involvement in the CDU on top of it all.

Somehow, I felt as though attending these events gave me additional strength and energy for everything else.

On Thursday, February 16, 2023, I visited my second "factory" in Berlin (#21). In my relatively short but intense career as an IT consultant, I had already seen the inside of three production halls. At one of them, I even got a tour from a quirky Polish engineer who, for reasons beyond my understanding, had a fascination with German cemeteries. He enthusiastically discussed the Hamburg municipal cemetery with me.

However, this second Berlin "factory," much like my first, had little in common with the production engines of our thriving market economy. Technically, the building wasn't even called a factory—it was Factory Berlin. Where a wheat beer brewery once stood, there was now an office campus for incubators.

An incubator is a facility where massive, soulless corporations— often with the government's help—throw pocket-change money at the wildest ideas, hoping to spark a profitable chain reaction. They likely also serve as a playground and occupational therapy for particularly creative individuals, keeping them from causing too much trouble in the real world.

At that time, there were at least two Factory Berlin locations. One was near Görlitzer Park, and the other close to the II. Sophienfriedhof cemetery. This confused me slightly, as the operating company didn't seem to bother giving the two buildings distinct names. I was already familiar with the attic of the Factory Berlin near Görlitzer Park from event #9, as it served as an event space for Code University.

That Thursday evening, I got to know the Factory Berlin near the II. Sophienfriedhof. As I wondered whether the nearby cemetery would have appealed to the exceptionally lively Polish engineer I once met, I found myself captivated by several presentations from the Californian startup RapidAPI.

As the talks progressed, metaphorical dollar signs began flashing in my eyes. Not only did they explain how to implement an API, but they also detailed how to monetize it effectively—a key part of RapidAPI's business model. Essentially, they offer developers a paywall service to charge for requests made to their APIs. In return, RapidAPI takes a small cut of the API revenue.

An API is what hides my ugly, junky code from other programs and allows other developers to use its functions. For example, someone might send a request to my API to find out the average rent on a specific street in Berlin. Cleanly formatted and without revealing what happens behind the scenes, my API would return a result.

In essence, an API is like a bridge between two programs—except you can't see what's happening on the other side of the bridge. Ideally, what's behind the bridge is an intelligent program that calculates the answer using Berlin's official rent index and other reliable sources. In the worst case, it's a dumb program that generates random numbers that sound plausible and sends them back.

IT professionals aren't exactly famous for their social skills, and I wasn't particularly appreciated for my irresistible know-it-all charisma either. Still, I was aware that social skills were something you could practice—at least in my case. With enough practice, I knew I could improve.

The IT events I attended brought together a variety of people. Generally, I met the more socially inclined and open-minded types of IT professionals; everyone else stayed home. This made the events the perfect training ground. I set myself the goal of interacting with at least one person at every event.

I didn't always succeed, but those evenings were rare. For every event where I didn't interact with anyone, there was one where I connected with two or three people. On average, I'd say I was fairly successful in achieving my goal.

Five days after my evening at the RapidAPI Penthouse (yes, that's what they call it), I found myself at Basecamp (#22). Typically, there's a 20-to-30-minute window before the talks begin at such events. During this time, organizers usually encourage attendees to grab a drink and mingle. The same was true at the meeting of the AWS User Group at Basecamp.

Since there didn't seem to be any interesting alcohol-free or sugar-free drinks available, I secured a seat in the front row and took in my surroundings. In the second row sat two guys chatting cheerfully. That evening, I felt relaxed and motivated, so I seized the moment and opened with my go-to icebreaker: "Are you both Data Engineers?"

After a friendly response from one of them and some back-and-forth to clarify their technical backgrounds, the conversation was off to a smooth start. As we talked, I quickly realized just how small the IT world in Berlin really is. It turned out that one of them and I shared a mutual acquaintance, and, as it happened, their children even attended the same kindergarten.

After a brief yet engaging exchange with the gentlemen, the talks began. The speakers explained how telecommunications systems could soon (and, in some cases, already do) integrate into the cloud.

The next three events (#23, #24, #25) took place at Taxfix, an online tax return software provider; at SIBB e.V., a Berlin-based industry association for the digital economy; and at Delivery Hero, whose office was just a stone's throw from Google's. While I really liked the venue at Taxfix (#23), I couldn't muster much enthusiasm that evening for React, the JavaScript library, or the topics related to it.

At SIBB (#24), I found the FinTech theme highly interesting, but the early start time of the event threw me off. As a newly minted early riser (during my student days, I would have breakfast at lunchtime in the campus cafeteria), I generally preferred events that began before 7:00 PM. However, 5:00 PM felt a bit too early and forced me to restructure my workday to make it fit.

One participant, in contrast to me, had the privilege of attending the event as part of her working hours. I couldn't help but feel a flicker of envy about that.

At Delivery Hero (#25), the talks were quite inspiring and encouraged me to think more about getting involved in Open Source initiatives myself. However, I was deeply irritated by the frequency and length of the breaks. I had never experienced anything like it before—or since. It simply didn't make sense.

If, as an organizer, you're more excited about the social aspect of an event, you're free to keep the talks as brief as possible. But why would you repeatedly ramp up the audience's attention for just five minutes of presentation, only to let it drop again for yet another socializing break?

Despite the somewhat disjointed flow of that early March evening, I left the event in good spirits. The peaceful night sky stretched above me, and I walked home with a spring in my step through Berlin's Monbijou Park.

Chapter 6 - Army of Zombies

For whom, and for what purpose, am I actually writing my event reports? Two answers battled for dominance in my subconscious, neither of them managing to claim victory so far. The first answer was: "For others, to convince them of my competence and abilities." The second was: "For myself, to actually become more competent and capable."

I had to admit that my need for approval was a powerful motivator. Of course, I wanted to impress my professional peers with the knowledge I had gained and the experiences I had gathered. Yet, at the same time, I sabotaged myself in this regard.

Having already written several LinkedIn articles, I was well aware of the usefulness of hashtags and tagging when publishing content. Adding many hashtags to an article on LinkedIn broadens its context and ensures it reaches a larger audience. In fact, I had observed that articles with numerous hashtags generally received more likes than those with few or none.

And yet, the vast majority of my event reports carried only the solitary hashtag #EventReport.

It wouldn't take much imagination on my part to add more hashtags. For my 26th report on an event hosted by the AWS User Group at the International Trade Center in Berlin on the evening of Tuesday, March 14, 2023, the following hashtags would have fit perfectly: #AWS, #PublicCloudGroup, #InternationalTradeCenter, #Serverless, #ML, #Lambda, #Berlin, #Friedrichstraße, #CloudWatch, #HuggingFace, #AWSCommunityDay, #SQS, and #Hyperscaler.

So why the hesitation? With hashtags of this quality and quantity, I could undoubtedly generate far more attention and likes. Yet, more than a year after writing those reports, my reports No. 26, 27, and 28 had each received a measly one like. Reports No. 29 and No. 30 had completely flown under the radar, receiving not a single like.

Even though I knew it was within my control to change this, I stubbornly resisted altering my approach.

In my mind, I rationalized this in a masterful way: while meaningful hashtags might help my event reports reach a broader audience, the audience would be different each time. My reports would lose their identity as a collection chronicling my journey through various events. Instead, they would just become contributions to an existing topic. As such, they wouldn't seem to me to have the necessary level of quality.

An even stronger argument was my paranoia. I feared attracting the attention of the "wrong" people—though I couldn't quite define who these "wrong" people might be or how they could harm me through my reports. On top of that, I didn't yet feel entirely confident (and to some extent, still don't) about my "Event Report" format. After all, I hadn't seen anyone else systematically create and publish event reports on LinkedIn in the way I was doing.

Even though I couldn't shake the feeling that my paranoia and insecurity were unnecessarily holding me back, I postponed making a definitive decision to some vague future date. Surely, at some point, I would know what to do. At some point, my paranoia would vanish completely, and my insecurities would be conquered.

Or would they not?

All these thoughts would, of course, become entirely meaningless if I were writing these reports solely for myself. There was quite a bit to support this idea. To write a report at all, I had to actively listen to the speakers at an event and diligently record what I heard in the notes app on my smartphone.

I enjoy talking, and listening has always been a challenge for me. Yet, as an IT consultant, listening is a survival skill. Clients never explicitly state their most critical requirements. Instead, they casually drop system-critical, make-or-break demands in passing comments or bury them in a PowerPoint slide in a spot no one looks at.

They don't do this out of malice. Many system requirements seem trivial and self-evident to them after years of working with the system. Furthermore, while they often possess extensive business expertise, they frequently have no understanding of the technology available to implement their needs.

At event No. 27, I had the opportunity to put my trained ear to the test. The challenge began even before the first presentation, as I had to navigate a maze-like courtyard with a construction site to reach the venue. Finding the offices of Kinvolk, a Microsoft subsidiary, was no small feat.

In general, I've noticed that Microsoft-sponsored events or those related to Microsoft topics were rare and difficult to locate in Berlin. When I did manage to find one, it often felt like a reverse escape room—where the goal was simply to make it into the event space. It seemed Microsoft took the phrase *"Only the tough get into the garden"* quite seriously.

Eventually, I made it inside and caught my breath, only to feel like I'd gone from the frying pan into the fire. The first talk was about running macOS Metal on AWS using modified Kubernetes worker nodes. It was vague and incomprehensible. Internally, I imagined the speaker connecting to AWS with an army of hollowed-out Apple zombie Macs and using Kubernetes to issue automated commands to the zombie Mac army.

But why he was doing this only became clear to me when an audience member asked a smart question at the end of the presentation. The speaker really should have started with the goal and motivation behind his topic. But perhaps he thought that was too trivial. After all, everyone must know that you can't build iPhone apps on regular computers—any iPhone app developer certainly does.

The speaker, however, was addressing Kubernetes enthusiasts, not iPhone developers—a fact that seemed to escape him in the heat of the moment. When asked about the purpose and motivation behind the entire exercise, the developer explained that the goal was to automate the build process for iPhone apps as much as possible using Kubernetes, and to accomplish this entirely in the cloud. Previously, this wasn't feasible because macOS Metal didn't exist in the cloud. In short, the aim was: more automation and more cloud. After this explanation, the audience collectively sighed in relief as the penny finally dropped.

At event No. 28, held on a street named after a knight from my home region, I was introduced to Pimcore, a product and customer data management software. I also inadvertently disappointed a Lassie-like dog when I had to refuse interaction with him due to allergies. The dog had enthusiastically run up to me after seeing me laugh, and it pained me internally to ignore him.

The very next day, on Thursday, March 23, 2023, at event No. 29, I listened to a surprisingly brief keynote presentation at the Berlin Institute of Health. The speaker remarked that the medical field had so far focused almost exclusively on imaging techniques in the realm of artificial intelligence, with significant catching up to do in other AI application areas.

After briefly mentioning Med-PaLM, essentially a ChatGPT for medical professionals, he concluded the presentation in under 10 minutes, transitioning the audience to the discussion and socializing portion of the evening.

The following week, on Wednesday, March 29, 2023, I attended my 30th event, hosted by Nord Security—the Lithuanian company behind NordVPN. Before the presentations began, I had a short conversation with one of their Senior Security Engineers. The Nord Security team then delivered a series of talks introducing their new software, Meshnet.

My five event visits (#26–#30) were accompanied by both a personal high point and a personal low point. The unofficial announcement of my promotion from Associate Architect to Senior Delivery Architect on March 13, 2023, was what I considered a personal high.

On the other hand, noticing a persistent and significant redness on my neck a week later felt like a personal low. Fortunately, I was able to resolve the redness two weeks later when I realized it probably wasn't the best idea to eat 200g of unsalted peanuts every day. You experiment, and you learn.

Chapter 7 - Ice Cream at the Beach

With indignation in his voice, the speaker opened the event by announcing that Google would be increasing the price of its BigQuery service by a hefty 25% starting July 5, 2023. A lively start to my 31st event, held on March 30, 2023, at Flink SE.

Flink is one of those "Deliveroo-for-groceries" companies catering to people too lazy to go to the supermarket, happily funded by venture capitalists eager to foot the bill for such convenience. One day, Flink SE hopes to establish a monopoly on grocery delivery and charge steep fees for it. That's the dream. And what will customers do then? Trudge to the supermarket for free?

As absurd as the business model may seem, Flink has an office with a fantastic event space. I was already familiar with the venue from the early days before my event-reporting odyssey began, back when I attended a Data Engineers meetup there. At the time, I didn't feel the need to document the experience on LinkedIn. When exactly it was and what it was about is now a vague memory—after all, I didn't have the benefit of a detailed event report to jog my recollection.

So be it—I still remembered that Flink had built its entire Data Engineering setup on Google Cloud. BigQuery is one of those Google Cloud services that's immensely important for Data Engineering, so the price hike would surely affect my colleagues at the discount grocery delivery company. Or so I thought.

My assumption turned out to be a bit simplistic. I shared the fun fact about the massive price increase whenever the opportunity arose during small talk with Data Engineers at other events. Through these conversations, I learned that the price hike wasn't as unfair as it initially seemed.

The first clue came while I was processing the event afterward—writing my event report. I couldn't find any mention online of a blanket price hike for all of BigQuery. Instead, the 25% increase applied specifically to **on-demand analysis** with BigQuery. On-demand means that whenever it suits me, Google has to conjure up a machine out of thin air and get it running like a magician pulling a rabbit from a hat. Google apparently wanted to discourage this practice.

As one Data Engineer at a video game startup explained, Google simultaneously reduced the prices for **reserved capacity**, meaning pre-booked resources. For those already firmly entrenched in the Google Cloud ecosystem, this didn't result in much of a price change.

It was, in fact, a brilliant move. First, they startled everyone with alarming news, then prophetically offered a solution that not only increased customer loyalty but also improved Google's resource planning. Chapeau!

In general, it seems as though cloud providers of all kinds intentionally design their pricing models to be as confusing as possible. This makes it difficult for developers to accurately predict costs in advance. I like to compare this to an ice cream vendor at the beach.

Economics or game theory students might be familiar with the *ice cream vendor on the beach problem*, which explores the impact of location factors. However, my analogy isn't about the optimal positioning of ice cream vendors on the beach—it's about the vendors' ability to optimally confuse their customers.

In my analogy, Ice Cream Vendor A (or Cloud Provider A) offers their ice cream at an enticingly low base price of 3 cents but charges 50 cents for every lick of the ice cream.

Ice Cream Vendor B (or Cloud Provider B), on the other hand, sets a base price of 10 cents, doesn't care how many licks the ice cream gets, but adds a 40-cent service fee for every 10-second interval the customer spends at the ice cream stand.

Now, if the mother (or the boss) asks the child (or the developer) which vendor (or cloud provider) offers the cheaper ice cream, the question leaves them speechless. They can only look bewildered. Instead of resolving the decision problem in an objective and rational way, the child (or developer) resorts to subjective, emotional justifications, raving about the unique flavor of one vendor's ice cream.

This allows the vendors (or cloud providers) to focus entirely on appealing to the emotional aspects of their customers' decision-making, since no one really understands the pricing anyway.

On Tuesday, April 4, 2023, I attended the event *"Spotlight on Cybersecurity"* (#32) at Y42. The venue was so inconveniently located that I was actually forced to take the bus to get there. To make matters worse, a sweet but aggressive dog decided it wanted to bite me in a very sensitive area. After successfully fending off the dog, I made it to the event space at 42 Berlin, a programming academy.

The 42 Network is built around a concept that aims to provide everyone with a free education in programming, free of any academic detours or complications. The training is funded by large companies with a significant demand for programmers. It's as if someone realized that good, reliable bricklayers don't need to study structural engineering to do their job. In this analogy, programmers are the

47

bricklayers, and a computer science degree is the equivalent of a structural engineering degree.

Whether this approach will prove successful is something we'll know in a few years—perhaps ChatGPT will let us know by then.

A day later, I found myself at Deutsche Bahn's Digital Campus, mingling with Angular enthusiasts (#33). There, I learned how to use a clever selection of TypeScript compiler flags to "force" front-end developers into writing better code. When the flags are set correctly, the compiler throws errors if it's handed sloppy, messy code. This forces developers to take another look at their work and improve it.

Six days after my visit to Deutsche Bahn, I ventured out on a rainy Tuesday evening to a dimly lit WeWork coworking space, where I joined a small group of Developer Advocates (#34). One of the tech evangelists present lamented the lack of meaningful monetary incentives or rewards for participants at recent Web 3.0 hackathons (Web 3.0 being an Internet built on blockchains). Instead, developers often received nothing more than pizza as a reward for their efforts.

At another WeWork the next day, on Wednesday, April 12, 2023 (#35), two developers from a hipster clothing startup explained the differences between Algolia and Elasticsearch. I listened intently as they described how to use a proxy to swap one service for the other with minimal impact on operational processes.

After the talks, however, I found myself in a real-life escape room challenge. I couldn't figure out how to leave this WeWork near Warschauer Straße on my own. In desperation, I started randomly opening doors, hoping to find one that led to the exit. Internally, I was already preparing myself for the possibility of smashing a window or breaking down a door if necessary.

Luckily, someone came along and showed me how to exit the building. It turned out that the exit was through an elevator. You didn't need to ride the elevator to another floor; you simply had to enter it and open the second door inside to leave the building. The elevator doubled as a passageway.

Shaking my head, I finally left this Twilight Zone of a building, thinking to myself that there was no way this setup could possibly comply with fire safety regulations.

Chapter 8 - Malt Beer Mix-Up

A common mistake that many developers, myself included, often make is placing too much emphasis on the technical aspects of our work while neglecting the relational side—or even pretending it doesn't exist. Yet, relationship-building is crucial. After all, it's usually non-technical colleagues or clients who decide whether to allocate a budget for our services. Even when the decision-maker has a technical background, they often lack the time or energy to fully understand the solution we've developed.

So, what do I do when I have to assess the quality of a developer's work? I rely on my gut feeling. And when do I get a good gut feeling? When I trust the person I'm dealing with.

I'm not a psychologist and don't claim to be an expert in human relationships. However, I've personally found it difficult in the past to ask someone for help if I didn't trust them.

How can I effectively build trust? Somewhere, some neurolinguists probably recommend adopting specific facial expressions or gestures, like always looking in a certain direction while speaking or using your hands to emphasize your words. Personally, I'm not a fan of these techniques. In my opinion, NLP and rhetoric coaches often make people feel less confident in their interactions, causing them to fail from the start.

My preferred approach is something I'd call "escalating small talk." In my first interactions with a new colleague or client, I make a conscious effort to create space for small talk, starting with topics like the weather or the weekend. These days, most colleagues and clients I meet understand the importance of small talk and are generally willing to engage.

50

If the small talk escalates, though—say, we end up spending 15 minutes discussing my counterpart's recent garden renovation—I don't cut it off. While this might seem terribly inefficient in the context of a single meeting, I believe it's much more efficient in the medium term. As we philosophize about landscaping, my counterpart gets to know me and my way of thinking in a familiar setting. Similarly, I gain a better understanding of their mindset. The result? Increased mutual trust.

I'm not entirely sure what mechanisms are at play here—and I don't need to know. My experience has shown me that the medium-term efficiency of my work and satisfaction with my deliverables strongly correlate with the quantity and quality of these small conversations. Plus, it makes my job more enjoyable. And that alone makes it worth it.

Once, I had the unpleasant experience of dealing with a team leader who considered any form of small talk a complete waste of time. She absolutely refused to engage in small talk with me or my colleagues. While she would give obligatory answers, she never allowed the conversation to escalate—not even slightly. Even the tiniest follow-up question about the weather in her area would be met with, *"Good, good. Now, what's the current status of your deliverable?"*

She would usually shut down small talk immediately, albeit politely, but it left me with a strong impression that she had no interest in me as a person or in my circumstances. This gave me the constant feeling that she was ready to throw me to the wolves at the first small mistake I made. As a result, I avoided asking her questions as much as possible and kept necessary Microsoft Teams calls to an absolute minimum.

I couldn't shake the gut feeling that, in her eyes, I was just a malfunctioning machine. Our collaboration was terribly inefficient. Many problems and knowledge gaps that blocked my progress at work could have been resolved in no time with just a little more trust between us. When the project under her leadership finally ended, I breathed a sigh of relief.

For me, mutual trust is central to fostering a healthy error culture within a team or organization. When I trust someone, I'm more willing to communicate mistakes earlier and more proactively because I have a sense of how they will respond. This shifts the focus toward fixing the issue rather than hunting for someone to blame.

In some systems, having the right error culture can be a matter of life and death. At the Health-IT Talk on Monday, April 17, 2023, I had the opportunity to learn about such a system in the elegant facilities of TMF e.V. (Technology and Methods Platform for Networked Medical Research) (#36).

A representative from a medium-sized Berlin software company presented the features of a medication management software to us. The software allows doctors and clinical staff to create and execute medication plans—in other words, ensuring patients receive the right pills at the right time.

Many patients suffer from multiple conditions simultaneously, meaning they already take a range of medications. The software checks for potential incompatibilities between new prescriptions and existing medications when creating a new medication plan. An incorrect mix of medications can, after all, be fatal. If the software detects a potentially dangerous combination, it alerts the user with a warning in the form of a pop-up.

However, this wasn't always the case. In the past, the software only displayed a small warning banner, which apparently wasn't sufficient to catch the attention of every likely overworked doctor. This oversight led to some fatalities due to deadly medication combinations. The software was then updated to include a pop-up warning, which remains on the screen until the doctor actively dismisses it.

While this case is tragic, it highlights the fact that no system is perfect and that systems can only improve through a transparent error culture. Most mistakes occur not out of malice but due to a lack of knowledge or extreme circumstances.

When others trust you, they're also more willing to offer constructive criticism. At event No. 37 the following Thursday, I couldn't shake the feeling that the second speaker might have serious trust issues with his colleagues or peers.

The topic of his talk, low-code, was super exciting and interesting. Yet there was no justification for cramming every single word and graphic ever created on the subject since the dawn of time into his presentation. The talk just wouldn't end. He simply refused to stop, even though the audience had had enough after 20 minutes.

If he had wrapped up at the 20-minute mark, everyone would have applauded, feeling satisfied and inspired. But instead, he carried on for what felt like an entire hour. Even the moderator didn't intervene.

Somehow, I managed to survive it.

Both now and even more so in the future, we will need to build trust in algorithms and artificial intelligence. Six days later, at the campus of the tax return app Taxfix, a CMO (essentially a CEO for marketing) shared with us that marketing professionals are already working to "persuade" Google's UAC algorithm to market their products and services (#38).

To do this, they have to negotiate with the algorithm as if it were a human being. Much like with a person, only through repeated interactions can they hope to infer what's going on inside its "mind." At least, that's the hope.

The next day, April 27, 2023 (#39), my trust in Google's navigation app was shaken for the first time. While the app did guide me to a location where an event was indeed taking place, it turned out to be the wrong one. The receptionist at the incorrect venue informed me that the event was for architects. For a moment, I thought, *"That works—I'm an IT architect, after all."* But then doubt crept in, and I asked, *"Do you mean actual architects, the ones who design buildings?"* The receptionist nodded, confirming my suspicion, and I left disappointed.

After another misstep that led me to the gates of the Berlin Gay Counseling Center, I eventually found the correct venue: the Malt Office on Wilhelmstraße 118. There, I learned about the Industrial Metaverse—a sort of *Sims* game for people who work in factories but would prefer to do so from home.

I also discovered the minimum daily rates established by Malt, a freelancer matchmaking platform. Malt seemed to operate on the belief that not every developer could be trusted to avoid underselling their services for little more than peanuts.

At a hotel right next to Bikini Berlin, I met representatives from Cloudflare on May 3, 2023 (#40). I was told that shopaholic, celebrity-obsessed tourists would be familiar with Bikini Berlin. Personally, the name only reminded me of Bikini Bottom,

SpongeBob SquarePants' hometown. Unfortunately, I couldn't spot the sponge-headed character anywhere.

Cloudflare is a company that seemingly enjoys everyone's trust, even though most of us are unaware of its existence. Around 80% of global internet traffic flows through Cloudflare. If the world were ever to end, Cloudflare would be the first to know. If Cloudflare were ever to go down, the whole world would find out immediately.

That evening, however, the world—and SpongeBob's shopping mall—were granted a reprieve. In a wonderfully pleasant atmosphere, an extremely enthusiastic Cloudflare representative explained how we could build our own Netflix in just 20 minutes using Cloudflare's Supercloud.

Chapter 9 - Polish Curves

Organizing an event is a monumental effort that requires a significant amount of time. Much of the hard work remains invisible to the attendees. Organizers must secure a venue, find good speakers, and choose a suitable date. The costs for the venue and catering usually need to be covered by a sponsor. The event must also be promoted through the right channels, or no one will show up. After weeks of stress, the event might still flop due to unfortunate circumstances. Even if it's a success, it's often forgotten just a few weeks later, leaving one to wonder if all the effort was worth it.

Attending an event, on the other hand, is laughably easy. A week before my planned visit, I filter the Meetup app by location and category, give a tentative RSVP, and then casually stroll into the offices of a company I've never heard of on the evening of the event. Sure, there's the initial uncertainty of walking into a room full of strangers. But that moment of awkwardness doesn't last long and fades away quickly.

Still, without the selfless dedication of organizers to host an event, none of this would be possible. So, how can a grateful attendee show their appreciation? My answer is simple: by writing an event report and publishing it online.

To make this easier, I even developed a structured format for such reports. My event reports always follow the same seven points:

1. **When**
2. **Where**
3. **Hosting Organization**
4. **Participation Fee**
5. **Agenda**

6. **Topics Covered**

7. **I've Learned Something Today**

This consistent format allows me to write a report in less than an hour without much mental effort. The last point, reflecting on what I learned, is the hardest to write because it requires genuine thought about the takeaways from the event.

If every attendee at a given event were to write a report using my format, the last point would likely be where most reports would differ. Everyone listens, learns, and takes away something different from an event. This usually depends on their prior knowledge and interest in the topics discussed.

In my ideal dream world, at least 10 attendees would write and publish an event report in my format after a successful event. This would both honor the organizers for their efforts and preserve the event's content for future generations. Perhaps it might even make sense to establish an organization dedicated to event documentation to promote this format globally?

Each event report could be converted into a machine-readable format like JSON, hosted on a code repository platform like GitHub, and analyzed in various ways. That's a vision for the future. Someone, somewhere, has to take the first step.

For now, I'll happily continue writing my humble event reports. Later, I can think about how they might be used—or whether they'll simply disappear into a digital drawer. At the moment, though, I feel like I'm providing a valuable service to the IT community.

I'm creating visibility for the remarkable variety of gatherings, topics, and venues out there. Surely, someone will find value in this—even if it's just to avoid repeating such folly.

On Thursday, May 4, 2023, I found myself once again at the AI Campus Berlin on Max-Urich-Straße 3 (#41).

The snacks were impressive—they even had mini brioche burgers. It's a pity I generally don't eat at events, but the food was certainly nice to look at. The overarching theme of the event was *Confidential Computing.*

It reminded me of a news article I'd read explaining how hackers managed to access foreign data stored in the cloud. To understand this, you have to know that in the cloud, you often share space on a physical server with other customers. Even if you don't share the same server, the machines are often physically located side by side. I vaguely recall reading about how some hackers exploited physical phenomena during computational processes to extract data from other customers in indirect ways. They didn't even need to break into the (presumably heavily guarded) data center. Instead, they simply rented a server themselves and ran some strange program on it.

Anyway, I enjoyed the presentations. That said, one of the Q&A sessions reached intellectual heights that my brain—already drained from a regular workday—simply couldn't keep up with.

The following Tuesday, I met up again with my friends from the Stream Processing Group (#42). This was the third event of theirs I had the pleasure of attending. Before finding the venue, I apparently woke a private resident from an early nap by ringing his doorbell and wandered around the wrong side street—just like the pizza delivery guy the organizers had called. During this detour, I met an AI expert specializing in computer vision. After thoroughly grilling him about the applications of his work, I eagerly listened to a programmer from Trade Republic.

Trade Republic is one of those neobrokers where you can also trade cryptocurrencies. From his presentation, I learned about the many advantages of the simple and unassuming CSV format compared to the more complex and elegant Avro.

Two days later, I found myself sitting on a well-worn couch surrounded by iOS developers, people who create apps for the iPhone (#43). The first speaker, like a mad professor, suddenly began projecting mathematical equations onto the wall and throwing completely incoherent sentences into the air. Although his performance as a frenzied scientist passionately sharing his love for cubic Bézier curves was wildly entertaining, I had no idea what the point of it all was.

After the event, I called a friend with a master's degree in mathematics and a strong enthusiasm for techno music. He explained that these curves are used to allow infinite zooming into any graphic without ever encountering pixels. That, at least, made sense.

When thinking of curves, I couldn't help but recall the Polish word *"Kurwa."* According to my Polish colleagues on the client side, the word technically also refers to curves—specifically, a woman's curves. *"Kurwa,"* I thought to myself in part when I had to inform them of my client transition. A change was happening at work: I had been assigned to a new project because I wanted to learn something new.

My previous client would have gladly kept me around forever, but I felt a little variety would do me good. Besides, I had the sense that I'd already learned everything I could in that role. The only thing I would truly miss was my colleagues on the client side. The humor of my Polish colleagues was unmatched.

Compared to my German colleagues, the Poles seemed significantly more relaxed. We laughed about almost everything. In Germany, people, in my experience, tend to impose far more limits on themselves. But yes, after a slightly *curvy* farewell, I moved on to a German client. Less laughter, but just as much action.

Luckily, I quickly crossed paths with another humor expert at the new client. Just as one fades away, a new one emerges.

Microsoft isn't just about construction sites. I learned this firsthand at an event hosted by the industry association SIBB e.V. on Monday, May 15, 2023, at the Microsoft Atrium located on the prestigious *Unter den Linden* boulevard (#44). For once, all the presentations were in German. The Microsoft speaker not only spoke fluent German but also demonstrated remarkable rhetorical skills. I was impressed and hoped to take inspiration from that for my own presentations in the future.

The following Wednesday, I traded the fancy atrium for a typical Kreuzberg bar for the next event (#45). There, I was introduced to a startup that manages value-added tax (VAT) compliance between various European countries.

A developer from either Google or Microsoft—I can't quite remember—gave a presentation on a front-end technology (web development technology). It felt like she was using the event as a practice ground.

This made me realize that this type of event is perfect for such practice. Before giving a talk at an expensive conference and potentially disappointing the audience, why not first practice at free evening events?

Perhaps I should consider starting to practice myself at some point. After all, I enjoy giving presentations, and maybe I wouldn't be half bad as a professional speaker—someone who actually gets paid for it.

Chapter 10 - Bizarre Dancing

I have a knack for systematizing and streamlining my daily life to achieve specific goals. As a teenager, for instance, I applied this skill to participating in postcard sweepstakes. Between the ages of 14 and 17, despite receiving a generous allowance, I could never get enough money into my well-padded fingers—a consequence of my excessive Snickers consumption. In my mind, an endless calculation was always running, determining how many video games and McCafé Triple Choc Cookies I could afford at any given moment with my savings.

At the same time, I was reading a lot of magazines, many of which frequently featured postcard sweepstakes. In these contests, participants send a postcard to a designated P.O. box, and the editorial team randomly selects a winner. After winning one of these sweepstakes and successfully selling the prize for a profit on the online auction platform eBay, I was hooked. I started researching online how to improve my chances of winning and decided to approach the process systematically.

I crafted a box out of a shoebox, writing my most important research findings as rules on the lid. Inside the box, I kept all the essential materials for "tuning" my postcards. According to my online research, Fortuna's role in the process was essentially taken over by an overworked editor. A striking and visually appealing postcard increased the chances of being selected by this editor.

Once I had set up my system, bringing clarity and structure to my efforts, I began to industrialize the process. I started fine-tuning individual elements to improve the success rate of a single postcard. Over time, my approach evolved into something efficient and scalable. The manual effort required to create a customized postcard decreased, while the average return increased. eBay benefited from the commissions on the prizes I sold, and I was eventually able to afford a Nintendo Wii—to burn off a few cookie calories with some virtual bowling.

By systematizing and industrializing my daily actions, I achieved excellent results in school, during my studies, and in the early stages of my career. However, two persistent problems have always accompanied this approach. First, human relationships and interactions are notoriously difficult to systematize or industrialize. To me, people are highly chaotic systems with far too many variables, and I don't consider myself an exception.

The second problem is that, at some point, I begin to perceive any system I create as a form of self-imposed oppression. With each day a system exists, I feel an increasing urge to completely dismantle and rebuild it from scratch. All my personal drama—and all my creativity—arises from this constant oscillation between order and chaos.

What am I getting at? On the weekend of calendar week 22, I met up with a friend with whom I can easily systematize our interactions. His actions are quite predictable to me because, like me, he has thoroughly organized his daily life and optimizes his time even in personal relationships. Let's call this friend Johannes.

The following weekend, in calendar week 23, I planned to meet another friend who has no control over his time. Let's call him Heiko. While arranging and carrying out the meeting with Johannes required only a few short messages, the situation with Heiko was the complete opposite. Heiko danced around the idea of meeting, avoided giving clear answers, and fully embraced uncertainty without the slightest hesitation. For me, it was pure agony. As a result, our meeting didn't happen that weekend.

I simply couldn't adapt my routines to accommodate his visit. I wasn't willing to throw my entire repertoire of weekend habits overboard for a meeting that might not even materialize. I believe most people operate like Heiko. But it's not because Heiko—or people of his type—are acting out of malice or don't value others' time. Rather, it seems to me that they undervalue their own time.

Admittedly, I only started appreciating my time—and that of others—after landing my first job after university. My respect for my time deepened significantly when I began incorporating time-intensive routines into my daily life.

Although people are chaotic systems to me, I still believe that maintaining relationships can be systematized and streamlined to a certain extent. Many people are even willing to adopt a proposed structure. However, one must accept that the process of forming relationships is inherently chaotic. Additionally, it's important to give others the opportunity to adjust to the suggested system.

For me, attending events and writing event reports has become my personal method for systematizing relationship-building within the IT community. By dedicating my attention and time, I aim to show appreciation for the contributions of those who organize and host IT events.

While the General Data Protection Regulation (GDPR) makes me hesitant to include the names of organizers or speakers in my reports, the reports themselves still serve as a time capsule. They document the activities of Berlin's tech scene and its contributors for future generations of IT professionals.

On Tuesday, May 23, 2023 (#46), a developer from inovex GmbH provided a service to all working Python programmers—and to me—that I won't forget anytime soon. He gave us a glimpse into a conference we hadn't attended.

A few weeks earlier, during my daily walk through Berlin, a poster featuring an octopus on a billboard stirred a pang of guilt in me. The octopus was advertising the "PyConDE & PyData Berlin 2023," a conference for Python developers. As someone who programs almost exclusively in Python, I felt a strong obligation to attend. There was just one problem: the conference, like most tech conferences, took place over three weekdays (April 17–19, 2023). My vacation budget couldn't accommodate it, and the ticket price was far from modest. Even the encouraging gaze of the Octopus Energy mascot, representing the conference's main sponsor, couldn't change that.

Fortunately, I managed to capture a bit of the conference spirit outside of regular working hours—and for the impressive price of €0. At an evening event hosted by inovex GmbH, I listened to a developer who had attended the conference. He shared his personal highlights, giving us a taste of what we'd missed.

Among other things, I learned about the new DataFrame library **Polars**, which is said to be even faster than Pandas. The explanation stuck with me: polar bears do, after all, run faster than panda bears. Additionally, I was introduced to the **WALD Stack**, a collection of open-source technologies for data engineers who struggle to "see the forest for the data trees."

Two days later, the agile segment of Berlin's IT community gathered in the stylish office building of SumUp, located behind the infamous Berlin Ostbahnhof (#47). While I did learn how to structure technical documentation using Diátaxis and how an agile approach can help navigate the dance with regulatory requirements, the true takeaway from the evening was of a different nature.

The moral of the story was clear: the agile world is dreadfully boring, and keeping one's distance is absolutely worth it. The agile evangelists masterfully tested my tolerance for mind-numbing monotony, pushing me to the brink of mental exhaustion.

That said, I was thoroughly impressed by SumUp's event space and its fantastic view of Berlin, making the evening, in the end, a success after all.

Five days later, I found myself in the strikingly empty halls of the Telekom Capital Representation venue for a few AI lectures (#48). Some stylish recluses would have done wonders for the place. In the nearly deserted, borderline eerie halls, I even spotted a few unoccupied gaming chairs. Now, that gave me an idea: Telekom could hire a few video game enthusiasts to hang out and game all day in their space. After all, it's people who bring life to a venue. Surely, it wouldn't be hard to find some students eager to combine a side job with their hobby.

Picture this: just before or after an event, you see someone chugging a couple of Monster Energy drinks and playing a horror survival game with friends. That would be quite a sight!

Anyway, this time my (data) engineer's heart got to race with excitement rather than die of boredom. I was particularly impressed by the presentation on lossless data compression—a method for handling the often colossal amounts of training data more efficiently. It was a highlight of the evening.

On Thursday, June 1, 2023, one of the hosts and I ended up engaging in an unexpected "dance" (#49). The prize at stake in this peculiar encounter? A bottle of sparkling mineral water. It had been a while since I'd experienced anything so odd.

After registering for the event, I felt an overwhelming thirst. Fortunately, I spotted the familiar catering setup typical of such occasions. Behind several large, transparent glass cabinets was a massive supply of beverages: cola, Fanta, beer—whatever your heart desired. My eyes locked on my target: a delicious-looking bottle of sparkling mineral water.

As I reached for the cabinet to grab it, a man suddenly jumped in front of me and asked what I wanted to drink. I stared at him, confused. Regaining my composure, I replied, "No worries, I got this." But he didn't budge and once again blocked me from opening the cabinet. My confusion deepened as he started explaining that it wasn't self-service—he would pour me the drink himself.

I glanced at the easily accessible cabinet containing my coveted prize, then back at him, trying to make sense of the situation. It was a hot summer evening, and my thirst only made his persistence more bewildering. A moment of silence passed, and then my mental "nonsense filter" kicked in. I looked at him one last time, smiled politely, and said, "Alright, nevermind," before leaving the catering area.

Later, as I listened to a lead developer from the startup Blinkist (an app for those who prefer bite-sized summaries over full-length reading) explain how they used ChatGPT not just to generate content but also to validate it within their solution architecture, it finally clicked. The awkward beverage service was due to the fact that they were only using one-liter bottles. Their intentions were good, but for someone who had never encountered such an arrangement in the 48 events they'd attended before, it was downright perplexing.

Next time, I'll be prepared. I'll skip the dance with the host and stealthily snag the water during the talks when no one's looking. Just as I did after my involuntary "dance" with the host that evening. As the saying goes: "Improvise. Adapt. Overcome."

Due to a business trip the following week, it took me 13 days to attend my next event (#50). The venue was an old GDR-era cinema called Kino International—a place I had walked past many times but never entered, mainly because of its rather unusual showtimes.

My 50th event turned out to be the pre-event for **Digisurance 2023**. During a presentation by a man who appeared to be highly skilled in PowerPoint, I learned that the Maschmeyer Group was exploring the InsurTech space. Together with InsurLab Germany e.V., they had even published a study titled *"10 Years of InsurTech in Germany."*

The IT architect in me was thrilled to hear about **Service-Dominant Architecture (SDA)**, a blueprint for building platforms. One of the platforms showcased at the event, **onpier**, was built on this very architectural foundation.

On my way home from the event, I stopped by my favorite döner shop and treated myself to a döner kebab and a döner plate (without fries). Then, I thanked God for my existence and my journey. After all, this was my halfway point.

Chapter 11 - White Monsters

I couldn't take it anymore. On the morning of Thursday, July 6, 2023, I decided to give up. Like the days before, my modest one-room apartment was already sweltering in the early hours of the morning. I couldn't think clearly anymore, and, truthfully, I didn't even want to function properly.

The past few weeks had been intense and stressful. At work, I was juggling the handover of my last project while onboarding for a new one, all while being pulled into the disaster that was a proposal creation process as a solution architect. On top of that, several business trips via ICE to North Rhine-Westphalia had completely disrupted my weekly routine. Then there was my master's program, where the initial excitement had long since faded, replaced by the monotony of churning out term papers.

Despite all this, I somehow managed to squeeze in IT events during that time. I even repurposed my vacation days the previous week to attend the Bitkom Congress *hub.berlin* on Wednesday (#51) and Thursday (#52). Dostoevsky and Solzhenitsyn kept my mind alive during these grueling weeks, but by the morning of July 6, my mental reserves had run dry. I was done.

I still had at least two hours before work started at 9:00 a.m. Ninety of those minutes were supposed to be dedicated to working on a term paper for my master's program. However, with my brain completely burned out and my mind utterly exhausted, I decided to give my overworked gray matter a break. At that moment, I knew exactly what a vacation for my brain should look like.

I got dressed, left my apartment, and walked to the nearest gas station. There, I treated myself to some mental wellness: a Thursday edition of the *Bild* newspaper and a white Monster Energy drink (sugar-free). I then made my way to a nearby square in front of a church, found a cozy-looking park bench, sat down, opened the can of Monster Energy, unfolded the newspaper, and began reading articles that were gloriously trivial and irrelevant to my everyday life.

The sunlight lifted my spirits, the energy drink banished the fatigue from my head, and the easy-to-digest articles in the *Bild* newspaper distracted my mind from the weight of my responsibilities. I went on to spend my workday with a calmness I hadn't felt in a long time.

The next day, I repeated the ritual. Over the weekend, I also freed myself from my usual obligations and fully embraced my newfound morning routine.

Over the weekend, I found myself relaxing more and more, and my creative spirit began to resurface. As in the weeks before, an ad for a writing competition popped up on Instagram. This time, however, it reached a relaxed mind that was open to new ideas. A thought began to form: what if I paused all my other commitments and dedicated the next three weeks to this writing competition?

I did the math and concluded that I could write a book in three weeks. The extra three weeks it might take to finish my master's program felt like a reasonable trade-off for the chance to write my very first book. The topic came to me immediately—my event visits stood out as the perfect subject.

That Sunday afternoon, in a burst of inspiration, I wrote the first four chapters as if in a trance. Over the next three weeks, my goal was to write one chapter each morning before work.

With each passing day, my mental exhaustion faded more and more. Working on the book reignited my enthusiasm. On Saturday,

July 29, 2023, I submitted my book, *Europe's Best IT Architect*, to the publisher's online platform for publication. However, it was rejected on the very same day due to formatting issues.

After some tinkering, I discovered that the chapter images I had generated using artificial intelligence were "too large" for the system to handle. I removed a few of the images and replaced them with quotes. On Sunday, I successfully submitted the book.

Afterward, I began working on my second book, *Airport Uncertainty*. I wanted to ensure that my first book wouldn't remain a one-time endeavor. While I had no plans to abandon my master's program, I decided to dedicate part of my time to my book projects. A few weeks later, I held my first printed book in my hands and saw it listed on Amazon. That moment solidified my decision to invest time in my newfound role as an author.

The height of summer, during which I decided to become a writer, unexpectedly turned into a "conference summer" for me as well. As I mentioned earlier, I attended *hub.berlin* and also the *World Developer Congress*. Thankfully, as a part-time student, I didn't have to pay the usual €300 fee for *hub.berlin*. Additionally, about a week before the *World Developer Congress*, I managed to snag free tickets to this similarly pricey event. *Fortes fortuna adiuvat*—fortune favors the bold.

Since both conferences spanned two days each, I ended up writing two event reports for each—one for Day 1 and another for Day 2, respectively.

On the first day of *hub.berlin* (#51), I strolled past a café on a sunny morning on my way to the nearest subway station, which would take me to the conference. As I walked by, I noticed a familiar face among the people sitting outside the café. It was a rising state politician I knew from the Young Union (*Junge Union*), who was already making waves in federal politics. There aren't many like him in Berlin—he's a relentless workhorse and exceptionally well-connected.

Buoyed by the excitement of my day off, the anticipation of the upcoming conference, and the crisp morning air, I greeted him enthusiastically and attempted some small talk. However, he wasn't alone, and it quickly became apparent that the man sitting with him was part of an important meeting. Somehow, I missed his subtle signals to wrap up the conversation quickly. As a result, I was met with a direct but polite statement: "Mathias, excuse us, but we're in the middle of a conversation."

Since I had initiated the chat out of politeness and was already in a hurry to get to the conference, I walked away unfazed, though mildly annoyed at my poor ability to pick up on social cues.

At the entrance to the conference, I was immediately greeted by a painting robot, which made me think of a painter friend from my hometown who once proudly told me about his under-the-table work. Randomly, my thoughts shifted to my brother, a civil engineer, so I sent him a photo of the robot.

After my first coffee—thankfully included in the conference fee—I took a seat in the front row of the conference's main stage and struck up some small talk with the person next to me. She later introduced herself as the head of IT for a major bank.

The undisputed star of the first day of the conference was the CEO of the Heidelberg-based startup Aleph Alpha. At the time, the topic of large language models was already a hot issue, so everyone was eager to hear the speech from the CEO of what many considered Germany's answer to ChatGPT. He gave a short, informative talk, but it wasn't particularly inspiring or charismatic. My impression was that he had stumbled into the language model field almost by accident, and when Germany's industrial spotlight desperately sought someone who resembled Sam Altman of OpenAI, it landed on him.

After his speech, I wandered through the other conference stages. Once I had reached my limit for absorbing new information, I left the event feeling energized and spent the rest of my day off unwinding at the cinema.

On the second day of *hub.berlin* (#52), I learned about the massive corporate database *Orbis*, which I would have loved to access, and a satellite startup called *Kayrros* that provides its clients with analyses based on satellite data. That very startup delivered a blow to my self-esteem during their presentation when they boasted about the number of PhDs and Master of Science degree holders they had on staff.

It was a clear reminder to stay motivated and complete my master's degree. After all, it's all for the noble goal of increasing the number on my employer's presentation slide under the "Master of Sciences" statistics by one.

Almost a month passed before I attended my next event, the *WeAreDevelopers World Congress 2023* (#53) on July 27, 2023. On my way to the Messe Süd S-Bahn station, I noticed many people wearing T-shirts with programmer jokes and outfits that made them look more like they were heading to Disneyland than to a business conference. By the end of the train ride, it became clear that these folks and I were heading to the same destination.

At the conference, a developer told me that his employer covered his entire trip and ticket as part of his employment contract. From conversations I overheard throughout the day, I concluded that for many participants, the event was essentially a company-sponsored school trip. For them, it seemed, the travel experience was at least as important as acquiring new knowledge.

The first day's highlights were worth noting. I learned how to use Meta's (formerly Facebook's) development toolkit to create interactive—but rhetorically inept—avatars for virtual reality applications. I also attended a workshop hosted by Finanz Informatik, where I didn't win an iPad but did get acquainted with the tech stack used by Sparkassen IT.

On the second day of the conference, I struck up a friendship with a developer from Istanbul during an observability workshop (#54). Due to a misunderstanding, he assumed I was a beginner programmer. Since I was feeling unusually unmotivated to engage in much conversation that day, I didn't bother correcting him.

Unlike me, he had brought a laptop to the *New Relic* workshop, so I spent the time watching him work instead of explaining that I understood more than he thought. On that note, I'd highly recommend the *iX* magazine. Although I wasn't an expert on New Relic or OpenTelemetry, I was able to quickly grasp the subject matter, thanks to having read the last 12 monthly issues of *iX*. Each issue, with around 140 pages, had thoroughly prepared me for the workshop.

The final day of my "conference summer" concluded with a workshop on Atlassian's Forge platform. An Atlassian representative spoke in lofty terms about the cloud-based ambitions of the creators of Confluence and Jira. Their new platform, Forge, which is powered by AWS Lambda on the backend, aims to make it even easier for third parties to develop applications for Atlassian products.

Exactly three weeks later, my "summer as an author" also came to an end. Routine had caught up with me again, though with one small but meaningful difference: I made room to continue writing my second book. To make that possible, I reluctantly accepted the prospect of a longer timeline for completing my master's degree.

On Thursday evening, August 18, a meeting of Kotlin developers brought me for the first time to the office of Volkswagen's startup, *Moia* (#55). The Moia office is located at Humboldthafen, a harbor basin offering a full, picturesque view of Berlin's main train station at the other end.

As a native German speaker, I find the name *Kotlin* for a programming language rather unfortunate. I probably don't need to spell out the associations it evokes. Kotlin is supposed to be the "new and better Java," and some even claim it's named after Russia's Kotlin Island—just as Java was named after the Indonesian island of Java. Geographically, Kotlin Island is indeed closer to Berlin, but in today's world, the perceived distance to Java seems far smaller.

That evening, I had the chance to listen to a startup founder share his challenges in finding skilled Kotlin developers. Despite these difficulties, the advantages of the language seemed to outweigh them so significantly that his company—one that had, among other things, developed a component tracking system for the German military—couldn't imagine doing without it.

Despite the success of the summer, I was glad to see it end. The oppressive heat had thoroughly scrambled my brain.

Chapter 12 - Socialist Code Dictatorship

I had just finished a long day at the office when I stepped into my favorite Asian restaurant (the name includes the word "Asia") to order two portions of fried rice with tofu. She caught my attention the moment I entered. While waiting for my order, my eyes kept drifting back to the young woman. Something had to be wrong—her face was buried in her plate as if she were unconscious.

I asked the chef how long she had been like that. He said she'd been in that position for nearly half an hour. Concerned, I tried speaking to her and gently tapping her shoulder to wake her, but she didn't respond. A teenager, maybe 14 or 15 years old, who had entered the restaurant after me, suggested that she might have taken drugs. He claimed someone told him she had used heroin.

I asked the chef to call emergency services, but instead, he handed me his phone, clearly unsure about how to handle the situation. Sensing his discomfort, I took matters into my own hands and made the call. While following the dispatcher's instructions, I waited for the emergency responders to arrive.

About ten minutes later, two ambulances pulled up, and around seven paramedics entered the restaurant. They took a more forceful approach to waking the woman, giving her a firm shake. Their efforts worked—she regained consciousness. Although she didn't seem particularly pleased, it looked like the situation had resolved itself safely.

After confirming with one of the paramedics that they no longer needed my help, I grabbed my fried rice and headed home.

On my next visit to my favorite Asian restaurant, I was met with friendly words of appreciation. Apparently, I had helped the staff navigate a difficult situation. It dawned on me that they must have been overwhelmed at the time, likely unfamiliar with the systems and processes in Germany. They simply didn't seem to know whom to call or what to do. It's even possible they feared getting into trouble for dialing the wrong number.

It might seem like a stretch to draw a connection between my experience at the Asian restaurant and the world of consulting—but that's exactly what I'm going to do. As a consultant, it's my job to help my clients out of tight spots. Much like the Chinese chef, my clients often feel uncertain. Both work hard, doing their best every day to keep things running smoothly. Then, suddenly, they face a situation they've never encountered before—something that disrupts their routine and leaves them feeling helpless. At that moment, they need someone who has been in similar situations and knows what to do.

As a former member of the Youth Red Cross who even participated in first aid competitions, I was able to help the Chinese chef and his guest with calm composure. Similarly, as a consultant at a major IT consulting firm with extensive experience solving countless IT problems, I can confidently and effectively assist my clients when they need it most.

As an individual, my time horizon is not long enough to encounter every possible problem and develop the skills to solve them all. Learning from personal experience is highly effective, but it's also incredibly inefficient. So, I dedicate part of my time to the next best approach: learning from the experiences of others.

The tech events I attend in Berlin are excellent for this purpose. Nearly every talk at these events presents the magical duo: a problem and its solution. This allows me to build a repertoire of solutions that my colleagues and clients can benefit from.

In calendar week 35 of 2023, not only did I earn my evening portion of fried rice the hard way, but I also expanded my repertoire of solutions on another evening. On Thursday, August 31, 2023, the *Forum Digital Transformation* of SIBB e.V. met in a WeWork office at the Sony Center to discuss the topic of digital sovereignty (#56). From a lobbyist representing a major cloud provider, I learned that it can be helpful to consult the *NIST Special Publication 800-53* if I ever lack the proper terminology or definitions for IT security in the context of government actors.

A week later, I had the opportunity to learn from a group of tech-savvy musicians how a music creator can make a living using NFTs (#57). While one million Spotify streams generate only about $4,000 for an artist, selling just 25 NFTs (digital merchandise) at $160 each to a small group of collectors can achieve the same income. Finding and convincing 25 hardcore fans to invest in digital collectibles— essentially valueless items—seems significantly easier than persuading a million Spotify subscribers to stream your songs.

Exactly one week after that, I listened to a young man with a French accent introduce an entire discipline designed to help companies manage their ever-increasing cloud costs (#58). In a stylish, somewhat old-fashioned office building (the lobby reminded me of the film *Titanic*), he demonstrated how *FinOps*—a blend of "Finance" and "DevOps"—can facilitate discussions about which IT resources are worth investing in and which ones should face budget cuts.

Exactly seven days later, I found myself at the SumUp office (#59). The office building is located behind the former main train station of East Germany (GDR), which, thanks to the fall of the socialist dictatorship, has since been downgraded to the Ostbahnhof and now houses a rather impressive McDonald's restaurant. The Stasi would no doubt have relished the mountain of data collected by SumUp's credit card terminals.

At the gathering of Kotlin enthusiasts that evening, I didn't quite click with the other participants, but the event still proved worthwhile. A Big Tech developer, who spends his free time contributing to an open-source project (free software), taught us how to use a code analysis tool to impose custom rules on developers. For instance, I could create a coding rule stipulating that any variable named **gdr** cannot hold positive numbers. If violated, the developer would encounter an error and, upon clicking on it, might see the following warning:

"A variable named 'gdr' cannot hold positive numbers because there is nothing positive to be said about the socialist dictatorship of the German Democratic Republic (GDR)."

Of course, beyond such playful antics, the tool could also be used to enforce company-specific rules with far greater practical value.

As expected, exactly seven days later, I attended the next event. This time, it took me to the office of Scandio GmbH on the infamous Sonnenallee (#60). While one end of Berlin's Sonnenallee is often portrayed in the media as a social hotspot, I found myself in a cozy office building at the other end of the 5-kilometer-long street. The event space offered an excellent view of the Estrel, Germany's largest hotel.

In a dim yet remarkably comfortable atmosphere, a rhetorically skilled speaker painted a vivid picture of the impending collapse of European civilization. According to him, the EU's *Cyber Resilience Act* alone would be to blame for this downfall. Despite the doomsday message, I found the speaker's presentation both entertaining and informative. Consequently, I left the office in high spirits after the event.

I had now completed a five-week Thursday marathon. Over five consecutive Thursdays, each a week apart, I attended an event and significantly expanded my repertoire of problems and solutions.

God, am I glad I don't have to live in the GDR!

Chapter 13 - Panic-inducing Boredom

In the fall, I found myself at the cinema. On a whim, I decided to watch two German comedies: *Ein Fest fürs Leben* featuring Christoph Maria Herbst (the actor best known for *Stromberg*), and *One for the Road* with Frederick Lau. Both films managed to evoke a sense of connection with the protagonists, even though I couldn't truly relate to their fates.

In particular, Frederick Lau's slightly pained yet endearing smile stirred something in me. It's a smile I sadly often notice in people I deeply value. It's a smile that frequently makes me pause for a moment, allowing me to feel empathy for what it might be concealing. Most of the time, I hope it's merely a physiological quirk and not the expression of some inner turmoil that cannot be resolved.

Mark, the protagonist of *One for the Road*, is an alcoholic construction manager who gets caught driving under the influence and has to attend a preparatory course for a so-called "idiot test." The film portrays the constant ups and downs of his life. Early on, alcohol fuels his social life. He has a lot of fun, and it's enjoyable to watch. But then come the inevitable crashes and problems at work.

As I watched the movie on the big screen, I thought back to how I decided after the first year of COVID-19 to stop drinking alcohol altogether. That decision, which felt relatively easy during the lockdowns, is something I still grapple with even now, after the pandemic has ended. Alcohol can bring a certain lightness to social occasions, and I do miss that feeling from time to time. At the same time, the beast that is alcohol devours an extraordinary amount of energy—energy I'd prefer to invest elsewhere. So far, apart from completely abstaining, I haven't been able to develop a sustainable system for managing my relationship with alcohol.

Despite the ever-present, well-stocked beer fridge that seems to be a constant at every IT event, I never touch the free beer. I'm usually glad if there are bottles of water or Coke Zero alongside the beer. During my second visit to Scandio GmbH on October 4, 2023, I grabbed a bottle of Coke Zero, took a seat in the front row of the event space, and started observing the other attendees (#61).

With one or two beers in me, it would have been easier to strike up conversations with others. On the other hand, I've always felt that social skills that only emerge under the influence of alcohol aren't real skills at all.

So, I glanced from my row of chairs to the standing tables in the adjacent room, looking for someone I could approach. I quickly spotted a guy wearing a T-shirt with a company logo, standing alone at a table. To exercise my social muscles, I walked over and struck up a conversation with him. He turned out to be an easy target, as I could simply ask him about the company on his T-shirt.

Speaking with a Polish accent, he explained that he and his colleagues, all wearing the same T-shirts, had traveled from Poland that evening specifically to promote their company's products. Two of his coworkers joined us at the table, and before I knew it, I was handed promotional materials and treated to a sales pitch.

My conversation with the Polish developer-sales team naturally came to an end as the presentations began.

Many participants at IT events wait until the end of the presentations and the official "social part" of the event to interact with others. By then, a few free beers from the obligatory drinks fridge loosen tongues, and the presentations provide plenty of material for conversation.

For me, that's not an option. I simply don't have the time to participate in the post-presentation socializing. To maintain my structured sleep schedule, I'm forced to cut short the social portion after the talks. Unlike most participants, who likely attend only two or three events a year, I can't afford to compromise my sleep every week as a regular guest at Berlin IT events. My master's program, book projects, and job would all suffer as a result.

That's why my "social time" starts and ends before the presentations or the official event program even begins.

This approach has three advantages. First, I don't have to worry about how a conversation ends. The start of the official event program quickly and decisively wraps up any discussion without concern for awkward exits. Second, it's easier to find someone to talk to. Many attendees sit and look around the room, making them easier to "approach" than when they're already engrossed in a group of beer enthusiasts.

Third, it prevents boredom before the talks begin. At many events, there's a gap of 30 to 60 minutes between the official start time and the actual beginning of the presentations. Organizers often don't share the schedule in advance. I've often arrived promptly, only to discover that the talks won't start for another 40 or 50 minutes. Other organizers are strict in the opposite way, starting the presentations right at the official start time.

In the former cases, I'm always grateful for a conversation partner—it makes the time until the talks begin fly by.

That Thursday evening at Scandio GmbH, I learned quite a bit about backups and how to prevent data loss. A skilled salesperson from a backup software company explained that the main cause of data loss is often not technically complex issues but simple human error. In some cases, disgruntled employees or those who've been let go deliberately delete data out of frustration.

We then heard from a Polish developer about his participation in a hackathon hosted by Atlassian, the company behind proprietary wiki software like Confluence. The first prize for their annual Codegeist Hackathon last year was an impressive $20,400.

After dreaming of striking it big, reality hit me with a nasty cold, and I was out of commission for an entire week.

By October 19, I was feeling well enough to attend the autumn meeting of the OWASP Berlin Chapter at the SysEleven GmbH office near Berlin Ostkreuz (#62). If I were a director shooting a dystopian film, Berlin Ostkreuz would be my location of choice. The train station building itself looks like a bleak industrial wasteland from the outside, making one question whether the triumph over planned economies was truly successful.

As if that weren't enough, right next to the station is the ultimate contrast: a modern organic food store brightly lit in warm, cheerful colors. The sheer intensity of the contrast makes the station appear even more dreadful.

It took a rather elaborate doorbell system to gain entry to the SysEleven offices, but once inside, the space was elegant, and the SysEleven team came across as friendly, approachable, and highly competent. OWASP, a global non-profit organization, aims to improve the overall security of software. Naturally, IT security was a key focus at the event hosted by the Berlin Chapter.

One of the presentations emphasized the importance of exercising greater caution when dealing with freelancers and managing access credentials. The speaker shared a story about a freelancer who had implemented an automated mechanism in their private development environment. This mechanism was designed to push publicly intended code to a publicly accessible GitHub repository. However, due to an error, the same mechanism accidentally uploaded client code that was not meant to be public.

Unfortunately for the freelancer, the code contained sensitive access credentials in plain text. A malicious actor's software, which continuously scanned public repositories for such vulnerabilities, quickly picked up the credentials. The hacker's program then logged into the client's AWS (Amazon Web Services) account and began spinning up crypto-mining farms to generate as much cryptocurrency as possible using "free" computing resources.

Fortunately for the freelancer, AWS detected the suspicious activity and halted the hacker's program before any significant damage could occur.

As a teenager with a creative side, I once aspired to join the creative industry. However, the movie *39,90* and a few articles about Berlin's creative scene dissuaded me. In my mind, I imagined competing with a group of out-of-touch millionaire's kids who could underbid me on every project simply because they didn't need the money. On top of that, I'd have to take drugs and adopt an unstable lifestyle—something I simply didn't want.

Nevertheless, on October 26, 2023, I found myself at the Spiced Academy on Ritterstraße 12, meeting the creative side of the tech scene (#63). No one offered me drugs or expected me to take any. Instead, the people there were eager to talk about *Framer* and their projects using it.

In essence, Framer is a tool for designing user interfaces for websites and apps. Since Framer can be integrated with code and offers some fun technical features, even I, a humble backend developer, found it worthwhile.

Five days later, I spent Halloween at the Google Germany offices on Tucholskystraße 2 (#64). At the *Spooky October Go Meetup*, I learned that the Go programming language handles errors in a way that reminded me of how I deal with awkward social interactions. Just like Go, I *defer* the next social interaction, *panic* when it becomes unavoidable, and *recover* after enduring the ordeal. The right combination of these three concepts can undoubtedly enhance the resilience of both Go programs and human relationships.

Let me propose a provocative hypothesis: "In Germany, there are at least ten times more programmers who primarily speak German at work than those who primarily speak English." On the other hand, I've observed the following in Berlin: "In Berlin, there are at least ten times more IT events conducted primarily in English than those conducted primarily in German."

That's why I was pleasantly surprised when, on November 2, 2023, I had the opportunity to discuss DevOps in my native language at the SVA offices (#65). As a nice bonus, I also picked up some background knowledge about the origins of the Kubernetes platform.

Chapter 14 - Pizza with a stuffed sausage crust

Code is code. I never really questioned why an app that runs on my Samsung smartphone wouldn't also work on an iPhone without significant adjustments. Surely, you'd just need to copy the code or program to another device, and that would be it—right?

As a high school graduate, I briefly tried programming an app myself. Using an app builder software, I managed to piece together a rudimentary "fun app." Even though the app builder hid much of the complexity of app programming from me, I still found the process too tedious and quickly gave up.

Later, as a student, I gave it another shot—this time without the help of an app builder. I bought a book by Rheinwerk that explained how to build an app using Android Studio and the Java programming language. I didn't get very far. On one hand, I lacked motivation; on the other, I lacked discipline. Still, I came away with an important lesson: every app must interact with its operating system to perform specific tasks.

The Android operating system provides different interaction possibilities than iOS. Moreover, even if two apps have the same functionality, their implementation can differ significantly, depending on how much creative freedom the operating system's provider allows. After all, one person's creative freedom is another person's security risk.

How frustrating and annoying must it be for developers to create an Android app, only to have to rebuild the exact same app for iOS? And what if I want to develop an app that also runs on a Windows PC or a MacBook? In that case, I'd have to build the same app four times! Thankfully, this problem has irritated enough developers that a solution has already been found. Enter the knight in shining armor: cross-platform apps.

Instead of maintaining a separate codebase for every operating system or platform, developers can now focus their efforts on a single codebase. Flutter is a technology designed to make this magic possible.

While other technologies offer similar tricks, on November 14, 2023, I attended a Flutter event (#66) at Revaler Straße 31. It was "first come, first served." On my way to the event, I noticed many people holding beer bottles. It was just before 6:30 PM, and they looked like they were heading home from work. Almost every second person had a bottle in hand, which struck me as slightly odd. Maybe it felt strange because working from home had made me miss out on my colleagues' after-work rituals—and I no longer had any of my own.

Back when I worked night shifts at a gas station between finishing high school and starting university, I had my own ritual: after a physically exhausting shift, I'd buy a small can of Mountain Dew and drink it in front of the TV. What Mountain Dew is for one person, beer might be for another, I suppose.

The event itself featured yet another "death-by-PowerPoint" specialist. Brevity is the soul of wit, after all. After the Flutter enthusiast bombarded us with a barrage of Flutter's internal mechanisms, I'm still unsure what his main point was. That said, I did learn how Flutter significantly shaped the app development of the delivery service Wolt.

Speaking of Wolt, it delivers the kind of things you'd typically grab from a late-night convenience store: popular items like Jack and

Cola, Red Bull, Coca-Cola, potato chips, and even "Exotic Whip Strawberry Flavour Premium Laughing Gas."

The following week, I boarded the S-Bahn to Potsdam. My brief trip to Brandenburg's state capital was to visit the Media Innovation Center Babelsberg (#67). That evening, the organizers impressed me on two counts: the event started on time and got straight to the point, and the entire evening was professionally recorded with high-quality camera equipment, accompanied by a skilled moderator who guided us through the program.

At first, I was a bit skeptical, as I had the general feeling that I was surrounded by journalists and media professionals who might not have much technical expertise. However, nearly every one of the three pitches and all three short presentations were packed with technical details. In one pitch, the speaker even touched briefly on the Kubernetes implementation behind their technical solution.

That evening in Potsdam, I learned about several fascinating topics: how the turn-key software solution Beabee supports community-focused newsrooms; how an AI tool automatically analyzes, tags, and distributes video content; and how AI could be used to improve reporting on domestic violence, provide real-time transcription for radio shows, support podcasts, and build advanced data infrastructures for investigative journalism.

A wealth of use cases that left me feeling inspired during the short walk back to the S-Bahn station.

Just two days later, on the morning of the last Saturday in November, I headed to a building at Humboldt University to attend this year's DevFest Berlin (#68). During the opening session, we were informed that the event would take place simultaneously in two buildings, a five-minute walk apart. The main venue, where the opening session was held, was located at Ziegelstraße 5, while the second location, another university building, was across the Spree River at Unter den Linden 6.

Since the more interesting talks were scheduled at the second location, many attendees, myself included, headed there. Finding the building itself was easy; navigating it, however, proved much more challenging. Even the on-site building staff couldn't guide us effectively through the maze-like and convoluted layout. After some trial and error, we finally reached our destination, though we frequently lost participants along the way—some never found their way back after a trip to the restroom!

Despite these logistical hurdles, I found the presentations technically fascinating and came away with many insights. At DevFest 2023, I learned how to use precise prompts to get Large Language Models (LLMs) to generate accurate GraphQL queries and how to control the input and output of serverless GCP services. Additionally, I gained valuable insights into techniques like Shadow Traffic, Feature Flags, and Beta Testing, which are instrumental in safely testing new features and continuously reducing the scope of regression testing.

On November 28, 2023, I returned to a familiar location that I hadn't visited in two years (#69). The Berlin branch of Deloitte, located at Kurfürstendamm 23, hosted a meeting of the Automotive Security Research Group Berlin, where we discussed how to design a security risk model based on vehicle diagnostic data.

Four years earlier, I began my career at Deloitte as an Analytics Consultant in the Forensic Technology department. Forensic Technology—the IT side of investigating white-collar crime—had captured my interest after reading an article in *Fraud Magazine.* At the time, I decided to become the best forensic investigator with a technical edge far and wide. The pursuit of economic crime sounded incredibly thrilling to me.

Although I left the company two years later, feeling somewhat disillusioned (largely due to my overly high expectations), I now look back positively on that time. I can't imagine a better bootcamp for mastering Microsoft SQL Server. I wrote database queries that spanned multiple massive servers, dozens of databases, and millions of records. I pivoted data in SQL as though I were working in an Excel spreadsheet and built complex recursive loops using dynamically generated SQL queries in stored procedures, treating SQL as if it were more than a simple query language and instead a full-fledged programming language. In short, it was a dream come true for anyone who enjoys working with databases.

The evening at the event was a success. I made several new contacts and left feeling a bit smarter. Although I initially thought I recognized one of the attendees as someone I had worked with at Deloitte, it turned out I was mistaken. Everyone I met that evening was new to me.

The Deloitte event space was impressive, particularly the Deloitte Greenhouse. Walking into it felt like stepping into a modern-day panopticon—a space that was simultaneously futuristic and immersive.

Two days later, I headed to the Deutsche Bank building for the ClickHouse Meetup (#70). While Google Maps guided me to the correct building complex, it failed to lead me to the correct entrance. Together with two other stranded participants, we tried to decipher the cryptic building map and asked both a puzzled-looking security guard and an exhausted office worker for directions. Eventually, we left the dimly lit part of the building complex, walked along the sidewalk, and discovered the event venue tucked behind a corner near a Netto store. My little odyssey took nearly half an hour.

Unfortunately, this shared experience didn't help me warm up to the other two participants. My usual icebreaker questions were met with curt and mumbled responses, so I decided not to pursue further conversation with them.

That said, the event itself was great. One term stuck with me in particular: Timebomb Query. A Timebomb Query is a problematic database query that performs well initially but gradually deteriorates in performance over time, eventually causing system crashes.

After the event, I walked into the Netto next door and picked up my favorite pizza with a sausage-stuffed crust. I couldn't have asked for a more successful evening for my 70th event.

Chapter 15 - Dark Woods

A new year had begun. As always, I had traveled to my parents' home in my hometown region during the days between Christmas and New Year's. For me, my hometown is a peaceful, uneventful village where not much happens, and I can find a sense of calm. Berlin, on the other hand, is the complete opposite. To me, Berlin is a dark and impenetrable forest, where chaos and the unknown lurk around every corner.

While the village feels safer, I believe it's only in the dangerous forest that I can discover what truly pushes me forward. That said, one should never underestimate the dangers that lie in wait in the forest. At the very start of the year, I got a triple dose of its unpleasant side.

To start, a fire broke out near my apartment building when a makeshift shelter under a bridge caught fire. This incident indirectly caused the water supply in my apartment to stop flowing during the day. As a result, I spent my day off at the office.

Two days later, on January 5, 2024, I encountered a mentally disturbed man who was coming from that same bridge. From a distance, I could already see he was agitated. I tried crossing to the other side of the street to avoid him, but this only made him angrier, and he began following me. He started threatening me because I refused to talk to him. Luckily, a neighbor—who had experienced the same behavior from him just minutes earlier—came to my aid. Together, we managed to scare him off.

However, we didn't let him simply walk away. My neighbor had already called the police, so we followed the man until the officers arrived and detained him. In hindsight, I realized that I had unnecessarily escalated the situation. While the disturbed man had no right to block my path, I could have simply listened to him with empathy. When he eventually stopped bothering me and approached a Lieferando delivery driver instead, the courier reacted calmly and just listened to him. The man wasn't nearly as aggressive or confrontational toward the driver as he had been with me.

Perhaps, in the future, enduring an uncomfortable but empathetic conversation might spare me from worse—like a knife in the gut.

The third unpleasant side of the "forest" manifested itself in the form of Berlin's icy, unforgiving winter. After finishing my studies, I swore I would never take the bus again. The one time I broke this vow, I immediately regretted it. The year before, I had taken a bus to my 32nd event, only to encounter a small dog that, for reasons unknown, seemed intent on expressing its disapproval of my family planning by trying to bite me in the crotch. That experience solidified my boycott of buses.

So, on Tuesday, January 9, 2024, rather than taking a bus to the inconveniently located Konrad-Adenauer-Stiftung Academy building, which wasn't well-served by either the S-Bahn or U-Bahn, I walked 20 minutes in the bitter cold from the Tiergarten S-Bahn station to the academy (#71).

Although I was thoroughly frozen by the time I arrived, the evening turned out to be worthwhile. The event was a panel discussion about Berlin's Smart City Strategy, originally developed in 2015 and updated in 2020. Thanks to an offhand comment during the discussion, I learned that page 84 of the 2023 coalition agreement between Berlin's CDU and SPD includes a plan for a Digital Twin.

A Digital Twin is a virtual model of a real object, system, or process that mirrors and simulates its properties and behavior in real time. In this case, the real-world object would be the city of Berlin itself.

At just my second event of 2024 (#72), Berlin's winter decided to up the ante with a potentially bone-breaking encore, far more threatening to my well-being than simply freezing on a dark but otherwise uneventful Tuesday evening. Two days later, not only did I put my physical safety at risk, but so did others as I made my way to the Berlin IT office of Mercedes-Benz for an event hosted by Kubernetes enthusiasts.

The entire city seemed blanketed in black ice. Every sidewalk in the vicinity of the Spindlerhof Berlin, where the event was held, was affected. Everywhere I looked, pedestrians were gingerly shuffling forward, trying not to slip. People were falling regularly, and I came dangerously close to losing my balance multiple times on my way. On one hand, I didn't want to arrive late; on the other, every brisk step on the icy pavement threatened me with a broken bone.

Somehow, I managed to reach Spindlerhof on time. After a brief round of what felt like a reverse escape game to locate the right elevator, I finally made it to the event. There, I added new software concepts to my repertoire.

The "Light Switch" philosophy in software design focuses on creating simple interfaces for complex systems, enabling users to interact with them effortlessly. Meanwhile, the Canary Deployment strategy involves rolling out a new application version to a small subset of users first. This group is gradually expanded to test the performance and stability of the update before a full rollout.

A week later, at an event hosted by the Berlin R User Group (#73), the biggest challenge I faced wasn't a band of rowdy pirates but simply navigating a dark courtyard that led to the venue. At last, it seemed that the Berlin winter had taken some pity on me.

While I consider R—a programming language for statistical computations and graphics—unnecessarily cumbersome and unintuitive (I'd happily see it retired forever), my keen ears still picked up some fascinating insights during the event. It was held at the offices of Reservix GmbH, a competitor to Eventim. There, standing in a relaxed pose and holding a beer with a friendly expression, was a man I decided to strike up a conversation with.

It quickly became clear that he was a platform architect, and in just a few words, he broke down the rough structure of his platform. The backend was implemented as a typical microservices architecture, with the microservices consisting of AWS Lambdas written in C#. After our chat, I realized just how dense the information he shared had been—and that I only understood it because I was already familiar with the concepts. This gave me an extra burst of motivation to continue my journey through the world of IT.

That evening's focus was on Quarto, an open-source software platform for publishing books, websites, blogs, articles, and presentations. The DevOps enthusiast in me eagerly noted a GitHub Actions workflow that built and published an entire book as part of its build pipeline.

Another week later, on January 25, 2024, I attended the next event (#74). This time, it took me to a place called Spielfeld Digital Hub. On the way there, I noticed the building was located next to a standalone McDonald's restaurant. On the McDonald's premises, I saw an American-style school bus, which appeared to be used for hosting McDonald's kids' birthday parties.

At Spielfeld, I met Web3 developers—essentially the Bitcoin version of programmers. Over the course of three talks, which primarily focused on applications built on the Web3 platform Starknet, my eyes were truly opened. While I had known there must be developers somewhere within the crypto scene, I learned that evening just how vast the developer ecosystem in this space really is.

On my way home, I felt inspired and began contemplating dedicating more of my time to Web3 development after completing my master's degree.

On February 1, 2024, I attended my 75th event, marking 75% progress toward my goal. Visiting the Scala Meetup was relatively straightforward, as the office of MOIA, the event organizer, was located directly across from Berlin's central train station. For me, this meant a short and uncomplicated S-Bahn ride.

At the event itself, I was in the mood for conversation. At first glance, however, the event space seemed full of MOIA employees engrossed in discussions with their colleagues. After scanning the room a bit more carefully, I found a promising target: a participant, roughly my age, standing alone. I approached him immediately. It turned out he was a Scala developer working with Big Data.

I felt an immediate sense of respect for him, knowing that Scala is the primary language used in Databricks. As someone who interacts with Databricks almost daily—but always using the far simpler programming language Python—I couldn't help but feel like a bit of an imposter in his presence. I thought to myself that the deeper mysteries of Scala were entirely beyond my grasp. So, naturally, I began peppering him with questions. Unfortunately, I didn't have enough time to dive deeper, as the first talk started shortly afterward.

The first presentation focused on Infrastructure-as-Code (IaC) and seemed highly relevant from a developer's perspective. However, the second speaker subjected the audience to what felt like a mathematical fever dream—something he must have concocted while dozing off in a math lecture.

On the way home, I couldn't help but chuckle at the dubious practicality of the second talk, but I was still pleased with reaching the milestone of 75%.

Chapter 16 - Fatal Christmas Tree

In my high school yearbook, there was a ranking section. Categories like "Greatest Athlete," "Most Likely to Become a Millionaire," and "First to Have a Child" were voted on by classmates through a survey. The top three in each category were featured in the yearbook. Aside from one classmate who managed to have her hard-earned title as "Biggest Chain Smoker" removed, my own placements stuck with me quite vividly.

I was particularly proud of winning both the "Teacher's Nightmare" and "Student's Nightmare" categories. At the time, I took it as a tribute to my rhetorical skills. However, it's equally possible that I was just very good at getting on people's nerves. That's something that will probably never be fully clarified.

In any case, I vaguely recall ranking high in categories predicting both a significant economic and political career in my future.

Almost ten years later, my contributions to the account of an economic career far outweigh those to my political journey. Nevertheless, after moving to Berlin, I resolved to become more politically active. For a time, I managed to attend political events regularly and helped with election campaigns by distributing flyers and hanging up posters.

Still, I found myself in a dilemma. While I had a significant interest in political topics, I saw far greater opportunities for growth and impact in my profession as a data architect. I was fully aware that my time, attention, and energy were limited resources, which made me feel like I needed to choose. In truth, I had already made the decision. My actions made that clear: outside of work, the overwhelming majority of my time was spent pursuing my management master's degree and attending IT events.

As a result, my political involvement in the lead-up to the court-ordered repeat of Berlin's Bundestag election on February 11, 2024, was limited. In January, I did help put up CDU posters across what felt like all of Mitte in freezing cold weather, but during the election week, my political engagement was ultimately limited to casting my ballot.

Instead, on the Thursday evening before the election, February 8, 2024, I attended a meeting of the Berlin Elixir community at the offices of bitcrowd GmbH (#76).

I didn't know anyone who developed with the programming language Elixir, nor had I ever seen a line of Elixir code before, but I figured I'd learn something new that evening. My hunch was confirmed when the first talk mentioned Big Data, which happens to be my daily bread and butter. Early in the presentation, the speaker introduced the seven Vs of Big Data: Volume, Velocity, Variety, Variability, Veracity, Visualization, and Value.

This reminded me of a time when I was rejected for a job because I didn't know the four Vs (the number of Vs can vary). Before I began identifying as a data architect, I used to chuckle at this anecdote, thinking that not knowing the Vs had no bearing on my programming abilities.

Now, as a data architect—and especially as a consultant with frequent client interactions—I see the value of the V-model. The Vs are a communication tool that enables me to have informed discussions with clients and decision-makers who are often not technically savvy. Without such tools, it can become unnecessarily difficult to build a bridge between the IT world and the business world.

A week later, I found myself wrestling with my own prejudices. The next event was to be held on Karl-Marx-Straße, not far from Hermannplatz (#77). From the media, I knew the area around Hermannplatz had a reputation for being a high-crime zone. However, a quick search on Google Maps revealed numerous nearby shops that seemed reputable and safe, so I decided to attend after all.

Once I got there, the area felt perfectly safe. With time to spare and nothing else to do, I wandered up and down the street out of boredom—and no one bothered me.

The event organizers made a welcoming impression. They seemed like a tight-knit community. As a relatively young consulting firm, the team at Pexon Consulting had clearly developed a strong sense of camaraderie. I especially appreciated how quickly they approached attendees to strike up conversations.

At many other events, organizers tend to ignore participants, leaving you to find conversation partners on your own. This approach can often backfire in the IT world, where many people are introverted and prefer to keep to themselves. Here, the proactive and friendly atmosphere was a refreshing change.

The Kubernetes-focused talks were bursting with enthusiasm. I also gained a new perspective on cloud platforms. As one of the speakers explained, a cloud platform can be divided into two main components: the Control Plane and the Data Plane.

The Data Plane, also referred to as the user layer, delivers business data to end-users or downstream applications. Meanwhile, the Control Plane manages and orchestrates the actual execution of programs.

Armed with new communication tools for my IT architecture repertoire, I boarded the U-Bahn at Hermannplatz and returned to my "safety-challenged" neighborhood unharmed and enriched by another valuable experience.

Not long after, on Monday, February 19, my next event took me to a quiet and peaceful residential neighborhood (#78). In stark contrast to the lively atmosphere of Hermannplatz, it felt like the proverbial "fox and hare" had already bid each other goodnight here by 6:00 PM. The only lights still on were in the office building of ML!PA Consulting.

Inside, in a cozy meeting room, I met members of the PASS Chapter Berlin. The PASS Deutschland e.V. serves as a central hub for knowledge exchange, professional development, and networking within the German Microsoft Data Platform Community. Essentially, it was the perfect setting for someone like me—a data architect who had completed all my certifications within the Microsoft ecosystem.

The evening featured a lengthy but intriguing presentation by an IT consultant who joined via Zoom from Austria. He introduced us to the world of Microsoft Purview, a tool designed to manage what's known as a Data Estate—an infrastructure for overseeing an organization's entire data portfolio across platforms and formats. The goal is to make this data accessible and actionable to support informed decisions and streamline business processes.

At times, the presenter delved a little too deeply into the details, but his enthusiasm more than made up for it.

A week later, on a Thursday evening, I found myself in the stylish and conveniently located office of a company I had thought was long extinct (#79). Surprisingly, some parts of their business had managed to survive into the Google Maps era. I'm talking about TomTom.

Before Google Maps became ubiquitous, TomTom's navigation systems (commonly referred to as "navis" in German) were a household name. Once Google Maps entered the scene, TomTom vanished from my awareness. I wasn't alone in assuming the company had been outcompeted by Google. Yet here they were, hosting a meeting of the Automotive Security Research Group (ASRG) in their sleek offices just a stone's throw from Alexanderplatz.

During the event, I attended a presentation about the process of establishing an ISO standard for vehicle cybersecurity. The speaker explained that while his organization wasn't required to make this effort—since there was no regulatory obligation—they saw it as a future competitive advantage. With the regulatory landscape expected to become stricter, customers would likely appreciate being able to offload their own compliance responsibilities onto their suppliers.

It was an insightful look into how proactive compliance could shape the future of the automotive industry.

Since moving to Berlin, it has almost become a tradition for me to take the entire week off around March 8th, International Women's Day, which is an official public holiday in Berlin. This year, the week coincided perfectly with the Transform digitalization trade fair organized by Bitkom, which worked out well for me.

Before that, however, my Instagram feed had been relentlessly flooded with ads for ITB Berlin, the world's largest travel trade show (#80). As it often happens, the ITB started a day before Transform, and tickets for trade visitors were surprisingly affordable. Moreover, the event featured an eTravel Stage, which promised content that even I, as an IT professional, could find relevant. So, I decided to check it out.

Once there, I initially got lost in the mind-boggling labyrinth of halls and levels at Messe Berlin. Fortunately, I managed to reach the eTravel Stage just in time to secure a front-row seat.

As a reward for my perseverance, I had the chance to attend a talk by a McKinsey partner. She presented some impressive figures about the size of the technology market in the tourism industry. However, when I took a closer look at the numbers on her PowerPoint slides, I noticed something odd—they didn't really follow any logical pattern. Instead of defining the size of the industry's overall IT budget with an annual metric, she seemed to have used cumulative values from a certain starting year. The whole thing didn't sit well with me.

Admittedly, the presentation, like many management talks, was fairly dull, as it lacked both technical material and depth. Still, after two talks and three panel discussions, while I didn't come away with any new technical expertise, I did gain valuable insights into the IT aspects of the travel industry.

One anecdote I found particularly amusing involved a mischievous programmer at a tourism company who thought it would be funny to "draw" a Christmas tree using letters, numbers, and special characters in a database field. Years later, this piece of ASCII art managed to bring an elaborate and carefully planned data migration to its knees.

I also learned that the Brussels-based lobby group Global Travel Tech would be officially celebrating its founding at the ITB in a dedicated event space. The head of the organization participated in one of the panel discussions and used the opportunity to invite interested attendees to the celebration.

On my way home, I couldn't help but wonder how many employees were behind this organization and what motivations— beyond the PR statements—had truly driven its creation.

Chapter 17 - Thirsty Machine

I stared at the machine in panic. My overzealous need for security had finally landed me in trouble. I couldn't properly open the cursed valve anymore. The machine sputtered through a few cycles, groaned in dissatisfaction, and ultimately refused to work.

Later, through WhatsApp, my practically-minded father explained to me that the valves controlling the water supply to a washing machine should be turned as rarely as possible. These valves aren't like regular faucets and wear out quickly. To him, my habit of closing and reopening the valve after nearly every wash must have seemed almost decadent. "Better safe than sorry," I used to think—what could possibly go wrong? Well, on this Friday, March 8, 2024, I found out.

Somehow, I managed to get the damned valve open just far enough to quench my washer-dryer's thirst. However, it was now clear to me that I couldn't simply close the valve again—I wasn't sure I'd ever be able to reopen it. From that point on, the Damoclean sword of my washer-dryer hung over me. If it ever broke down, I'd have to close the valve and likely replace it entirely through my landlord. Thoughts of how long that process might take and what it would involve haunted me all weekend.

Being on my own in Berlin, I couldn't simply make a ten-hour trip to my parents' house to do my laundry. In the end, for the sake of my peace of mind, I decided to simply throw money at the problem if it ever arose.

The week had actually started off well. After my visit to ITB Berlin, I attended Transform, Bitkom's largest annual event, for two consecutive days. On the first day, I was thoroughly confused by the

IBM team during an AI workshop due to their extremely liberal use of the term IP (#81). In the context of what they were saying, it didn't seem to make any sense.

To me, IP stood for Internet Protocol (Address)—a unique identifier for a device. However, they were talking about companies not wanting to make their IP public. When I asked for clarification, it turned out they were referring to Intellectual Property. Suddenly, everything made sense.

In the context of large language models like ChatGPT, few people care about the technical specifics of network traffic, but intellectual property is certainly a hot topic. Intellectual property includes things like books, texts, and articles—without vast quantities of these, it would be hard to train models like ChatGPT effectively. It was also understandable that companies would be reluctant to share their intellectual property, including trade secrets, freely with the public.

This, however, is precisely the risk posed by large language models trained within companies. With a few clever tricks, even a mathematically clueless hacker could potentially manipulate a model into "spilling the beans," exposing all sorts of trade secrets to the outside world.

The next morning, an FDP politician catapulted me back to my university debating club days at Saarland University (#82). Marco Buschmann, the Federal Minister of Justice for Germany, delivered the opening keynote for the second day of the Transform conference. He spoke about digitalization and reducing bureaucracy.

The articulate and highly dynamic Justice Minister captured my full attention when he began telling the audience about the metric of "Erfüllungsaufwand" (compliance burden). My former debate coach, who is now actively shaping the business side of Germany's emerging cannabis industry, always used to say: "To win a debate, you must present me, as the judge, with a clear success metric and explain how your arguments contribute to it."

Incidentally, my debate coach always wore a hat that reminded me of the eccentric billionaire from *Jurassic Park*. Who knows— maybe he'll build a theme park with stoned dinosaurs in my lifetime. Or maybe not.

In any case, Marco Buschmann demonstrated with masterful competence how to calculate compliance burden and how his efforts as minister were reducing it. In a debate competition, he would have been a formidable opponent with that level of performance.

On the second and final day of the conference, nationwide train strikes caused uncertainty among participants, as most had traveled by ICE from other parts of Germany. Many were wondering how they would get home.

Surprisingly, Bitkom demonstrated active empathy and organized FlixBuses to transport attendees from the venue to the main train stations in Hamburg, Munich, Cologne, and Frankfurt am Main. From there, it would be relatively easy to complete the journey home using local public transport or a taxi.

This thoughtful gesture, announced by Bitkom at the start of the final conference day, saved the mood of the event. Thanks to their proactive approach, attendees were able to enjoy the second day without the burden of worrying about their return journey. That day, Bitkom taught me the true meaning of hospitality.

On March 19, 2024, just under two weeks later, I found myself heading once again to Berlin's most dreadful train station (#83). After stepping off the S-Bahn and being enveloped once more by the dystopian atmosphere of Ostkreuz Station, I passed the brightly lit organic supermarket—a "city on a hill" that seemed to embody the promise of a better, idealized life. From there, I walked down Revaler Straße to the Thoughtworks office.

Here, I encountered a crowd that no developer truly enjoys dealing with: Quality Assurance (QA) specialists. QA, or quality assurance, is a necessary evil to iron out the worst software bugs. Still, no developer is thrilled when a group of nitpicky perfectionists rigorously examines their code.

The unofficial prophet of the QA world is W. Edwards Deming, the most well-known advocate of statistical quality control. His contributions even earned him the status of a national hero in Japan, a country with an extraordinary commitment to quality.

That evening, I was introduced to a metric that could help in managing a development team. The metric measures how often code is sent back from QA to DEV—essentially tracking how frequently submitted code, after being reviewed by the quality assurance team, is returned to developers for fixes. Like any metric, this one can have unintended consequences and should be used thoughtfully.

After a three-week break, during which I took a brief trip to Turkey, coinciding with the country's nationwide municipal elections, the time had come again on April 9, 2024: I attended another event hosted by the MLOps community of my esteemed nemesis (#84). Unfortunately—or perhaps I should say fortunately—my nemesis was unable to attend that evening. I learned this from a former colleague who had recently found a new home working for the competitor company DB Systel. She seemed to enjoy her new role.

Much as I loathe admitting it, the community supported by my nemesis once again delivered a solid performance. The event was interactive without being overbearing, packed with intriguing tech content, and carried a lively, relaxed atmosphere. Clearly, he must be doing something right with his involvement in this tight-knit group.

What stood out most to me was a talk on chunking in the context of large language models. The word "chunking" instantly triggered memories of KitKat Chunkys. As a high school student and later as a university student, I had devoured those oversized chocolate bars in absurd quantities. My brain must have unearthed this memory in a cunning attempt to get me to break my four-year-old vow and start stuffing myself with sweets again. This time, however, I resisted the temptation.

Six days later, I found myself wandering, slightly lost and confused, once again from the Friedrichstraße S-Bahn station to Charlottenstraße 42. My destination this time was the premises of TMF e.V. (Technology and Methods Platform for Networked Medical Research) to attend the 158th Health IT Talk (#85). It was quite remarkable that these distinguished individuals had already convened 158 times on this one specific overarching topic, while I, with my topic-free event visits, was just brushing against number 85. Perhaps I could learn something from their example, I thought to myself. There might indeed be benefits to focusing entirely on a single subject. On the other hand, my focus was already on IT architecture, so I felt I might already be on the right track.

That evening, I encountered four new concepts:

1. I learned of the existence of a specific section in the penal code that defines computer sabotage.
2. I gained insight into the importance of network diagrams—often neglected but critical in the event of a cybersecurity incident.

3. I picked up on the fact that the BSI (the German Federal Office for Information Security) maintains a list of qualified companies capable of providing support in the event of cyberattacks.
4. Finally, the dots connected when I came across the term PDCA cycle—a four-phase process (Plan, Do, Check, Act) aimed at the continuous improvement of systems.

Although the proverbial washer-dryer "sword of Damocles" still loomed over my head, my event attendance gradually helped diminish my preoccupation with it.

Chapter 18 - Inescapable Poetry

During my usual walks through Berlin-Mitte, a movie poster once again caught my eye, and this time, the theme seemed far from implausible. Intrigued, I decided to head to the cinema in the penultimate week of April 2024 to watch the film. From start to finish, I was riveted to the screen. The movie turned out to be a masterpiece.

As a viewer, I followed the journey of a war photographer on her path to the final battle of a civil war raging on American soil. What made it even more striking was that the story of this civil war wasn't set in the past but in the near future. In Alex Garland's feature film *Civil War,* we witness the photographer navigating her way through a war-torn America, capturing moments with her camera that are almost unbearably harrowing in their brutality.

Somehow, this vaguely reminded me of my event visits, as the events themselves are difficult to truly encapsulate. Trying to condense the wealth of information and interactions into a short LinkedIn article that takes no more than two minutes to read often feels like a futile effort. Yet, I think the same mechanism is at play here as with photographs. A photo without context holds no value. Only the people viewing the photo give it meaning through their own knowledge and experiences.

For me personally, every event report is like a portal to an evening where, as a young, naive, and still inexperienced software architect, I attended a gathering to listen to people who knew more than I did. On some evenings, I wandered aimlessly to the venue because Google Maps failed me. On others, I encountered attendees who blocked my attempts to make small talk. Some talks were dreadfully boring, while others made my young developer heart leap with excitement.

It surprises me how effortlessly I can transport myself back to those evenings just by reading an event report, reliving the atmosphere and experiencing it all over again.

When I look at my 86th event report and see the title image of an iceberg with penguins on it, I'm reminded of how I waddled through Ostbahnhof toward the SumUp building, took the elevator up, and stepped onto the still-empty event space. The brief frustration I felt when I asked the event organizers when the talks would begin—and learned it would be another 45 minutes—is vividly back in my mind. The impulse that followed, to use the time productively by approaching another attendee and striking up a conversation, resurfaces as I read through the report.

I also recall the impression my conversation partner gave me— that while he was intelligent and competent, he had a tendency to overcomplicate things and was generally dissatisfied with his overall life situation. That feeling pops back into my consciousness as if it had only just happened.

Even as I go through the "I've learned something today" section, with its objectively presented bullet points, each one stirs the thoughts or emotions that led me to see value in these insights. Why did I find it so fascinating to learn that the traditional approach to data integration relies on database dumps and orchestrated data flows? Because I had witnessed this approach firsthand in my work without having the breadth of experience to recognize it as traditional.

My 87th event report about a meeting of Flutter developers takes me back to the evening when I first ended up at the door of the wrong meetup before finally finding the correct entrance to the university building. Looking at the photo I added to the report, I vividly remember sitting alone in the front row of a lecture hall, waiting for the talks to begin.

I recall how, that evening, I was in no mood for conversation and didn't actively try to connect with anyone. Nor did anyone seem to approach me. Despite this, I felt captivated by the technical content of the talks and was thrilled to learn about the concept of Flutter's Gesture Arena.

My 88th event report, about a gathering of data experts discussing unstructured data in the context of large language models, plays like a movie in my mind's eye. As I ride the elevator up, I strike up a conversation with another attendee. He chats with me briefly but doesn't seem particularly invested in the conversation. When we reach the top, he cuts the conversation short and immediately rushes off to join his group of friends—his real objective. I don't hold it against him; I likely would have done the same if I had known anyone at the event.

I take a seat in the audience and listen to several talks about large language models. The scale of the technical ecosystem surprises me a bit. During the final presentation, the data scientist presenting briefly mentions his hobby as a poet. *Typical,* I think to myself. Skilled speakers often begin their presentations with a short introduction, sharing a personal detail to make themselves memorable. These personal touches also serve as icebreakers for later conversations.

On my way home, I reflect on the presenter's poetic activities. There's something appealing about the idea of writing poetry on the side as a developer. Perhaps one day, I'll try it myself.

My 89th event report takes me back to not just one, but two evenings of my Berlin misadventures. On the evening of May 21,

2024, I took an S-Bahn, exhausted, to the other side of the city, only to find myself standing in front of locked doors with no trace of the event I was expecting. A quick glance at my Meetup app revealed the truth: the Data Mesh event hosted by Kleinanzeigen was scheduled for the following evening. Frustrated but forgiving toward a Mathias worn out from a productive week, I headed back home, sipping on a Coke Zero I bought at the S-Bahn station as a small consolation.

How I managed to motivate myself to try again the next day, I don't know. Somehow, I dragged myself to the Kleinanzeigen & mobile.de office building once more. This time, someone was actually standing at the entrance, waiting to greet guests. A host led us through multiple floors, stairs, and elevators to the far end of the building. Upon arriving at the event space, I immediately knew there was no way I'd find my way back out on my own. This suspicion was confirmed when, at the start of the event, we were told that anyone wishing to leave early would need to ask a host to guide them out.

This announcement did not sit well with me. I've had the displeasure of being unable to leave an event independently before, and it stirs a deep-seated anxiety within me. There must be something primal about not wanting to feel trapped. While I can endure it, if given a choice between two events, I will always pick the one where I'm free to leave on my own terms.

Still, the event was worth attending. A glance at my event report confirms it. While it was somewhat light on technical content, I gained a lot from a rhetorical perspective. One panel discussion participant, in particular, impressed me with his eloquence. Half of my report is filled with quotes from him.

Who has the best office in Berlin? My 90th event report, about a DevOps meetup on May 30, 2024, answers that question: the clear winner is Cisco Systems GmbH. Cisco, a long-established heavyweight and the first company that comes to mind when talking about computer networks, boasts breathtaking 360-degree views of Bahnhof Zoo and its surroundings from its 12th-floor offices. I can imagine how delightful it must be to sip morning coffee with a colleague while watching trains come and go.

Before the talks began, I managed to connect with two backend engineers. They both enjoyed laughing, and I love cracking jokes, so we hit it off with plenty of jokes and loud laughter. They playfully guided me through the application landscape of their employer. Unfortunately, networking with them didn't go far—neither had a LinkedIn account, and I had long since forgotten my Xing password.

During the presentations, I learned more about the differences between DevOps and Site Reliability Engineering, the infamous Kubernetes warning message *DNSConfigForming*, and Cisco's recent corporate acquisitions. I left Cisco's offices satisfied, happy that I didn't need to ask the organizer for assistance, as I had at the previous event. With a spring in my step, I headed home contentedly.

Chapter 19 - Lightbulb Peninsula

It is no longer a given that people regularly and willingly gather in one place to discuss something or spend time together with strangers. This isn't due to COVID-19—I noticed it as far back as my university debating club days at Saarland University. Officially, we had enough members to fill two debate rooms every week. In reality, however, attendance was inconsistent. On more than one evening, I found myself standing alone in our modern seminar room at the Center for Bioinformatics.

While the frustration of those moments was sometimes significant, I couldn't blame anyone. I wasn't any better—I acted the same way in other contexts. This kind of problem likely didn't arise in the past simply because people had no other way to connect with others. Back then, you couldn't find and contact like-minded individuals with just a few clicks on the internet. You had to go where others went. Today, that's no longer the case.

Still, I see tremendous value in in-person events. Making the effort to get up, brush your teeth, put on reasonably presentable clothes, and embark on the often arduous journey from the comfort of your couch to a physical venue brings a unique quality to human interaction. Standing face-to-face with another person, perceiving them directly rather than through a meeting app, changes communication dynamics and generally makes people more open and honest. In a chat window with the camera off, it's easy to put on a facade, but in person, I am exposed to others exactly as I am—for better or worse.

Soon, we will be at the mercy of bots and AI in the digital space—for better or worse. In some ways, we already are. Long before the rise of ChatGPT, bots posing as humans were influencing our opinions with cleverly crafted posts. Today, I can no longer be entirely sure whether I'm interacting with a real person or not. AI can already handle chatting, and it won't be long before they master video interactions as well.

The last remaining way to determine if I'm truly interacting with a human seems to be in-person events. The ill-fitting shirt, the uncertain gaze, the shyness around others, or the faint smell of sweat from a long workday—these may be our final clues that someone is human and not an AI.

Why is it important to communicate with other people at all? A large language model chatters away without having any personal connection to the content it produces. It hasn't had to suffer to acquire the information, nor has it felt joy or satisfaction in sharing it. Moreover, it has infinite time and experiences no pain when spreading useless information. It doesn't care in the slightest whether it wastes computational resources communicating irrelevant content. Neither audience rejection nor approval motivates it to perform better.

So when someone chooses to spend their precious time on Earth sharing something with me, I see it as an indicator that the information might actually have value. Even more so if that person is willing to risk embarrassing themselves in front of others. That, to me, deserves more attention than a soulless AI, which at worst wastes a bit of processing time.

That's why, on the evening of Thursday, June 6, 2024, I didn't join an anonymous mass Zoom call. Instead, I went to the very real SAP Data Space on Rosenthaler Straße 38 in Berlin (#91). Upon arrival, after completing registration, I was mildly annoyed to discover I had 40 minutes to kill before the talks began—a perfect opportunity to get to know the other attendees better. After reserving a seat in the front row, I noticed a human intelligence in the second row. My counterpart appeared to have come alone, so I casually seized the chance to strike up a conversation.

The time flew by as we talked, and I even managed to pick up a bit of new knowledge about health startups.

Then the presentations began. From the first talk, given by an SAP employee, and the questions directed at him, I gained some insight into SAP's initial experiments with AI systems based on tabular data. However, it seemed that nothing particularly concrete had come from these efforts yet. Notably, these first steps were taken in collaboration with Merantix, a highly active organizer of events at the Berlin AI Campus. This brought to mind a presentation by a bright-eyed AI expert from Merantix that I attended on January 11, 2023 (#14).

Ultimately, the SAP representative shared a handy rule of thumb for estimating the inference costs of a model, which naturally found its way into my event report.

The other presentation of the evening drew my attention to a company called Jina AI, which appears to be a competitor to OpenAI. The data scientist representing the company praised Jina AI's embedding model, highlighting its superior performance and lower costs compared to other embeddings, such as those from OpenAI.

Five days later, I made my way to the somewhat tucked-away event space at Adesso's Berlin branch (#92). After crossing the office building's lobby and passing a Beets & Roots restaurant, I mistakenly assumed that I needed to head back outside to the second entrance in the courtyard, where oversized Adesso banners were prominently displayed. Instead, I discovered that the event space was actually located in the first building, hidden behind an inconspicuous wall that I initially overlooked.

Unlike the light bowls and salads offered by Beets & Roots in the same building, the evening served up something much heavier. The topic of the night was networks—not the human kind that occasionally require a "thumbs up" on LinkedIn, but the brutally complex ones responsible for making my application throw mysterious errors.

For microservices—essentially tiny applications—a service mesh like Istio can manage network traffic. The supposedly cool part is that, as an application developer, I don't have to deal with boring nerd stuff like the physical network structure. Sure, I'm a bit of a nerd myself, but I've never ventured deep enough into the IT basement to feel comfortable with such arcane wizardry.

Since this Adesso event was hosted by the AWS User Group, the open-source infrastructure Istio was naturally just the starting point to introduce the real flagship solution: Amazon VPC Lattice. As a paid service, it of course boasts far more advantages. By focusing on automation, it reduces operational overhead and eliminates the need for extensive network expertise. This makes it easier for pseudo-nerds like me to deploy and manage modern application architectures across various environments like Kubernetes, EC2, and serverless services.

Of course, a profit-driven corporation doesn't pull me out of my self-inflicted ignorance for free, so I'd probably have to pay a significant amount for the privilege. But since I have no idea how much I'd actually be charged, I'd likely max out the company credit card until some ruthless McKinsey consultant pulls the plug and shuts down my department. Eat, overspend, and get downsized by an overpriced management consultant—just the natural cycle of corporate life.

A week later, I walked down Friedrichstraße, now reopened to car traffic, heading to the Berlin office of the successful Turkish startup Trendyol to attend a meeting of Elasticsearch Berlin, a group for full-text search engine enthusiasts (#93). I was in good spirits, the *WELT* hot air balloon hung in the sky, and the folks at Trendyol seemed quite relaxed.

After the usual small talk with a few developers standing around, the first presentation began. The technical content immediately captured my undivided attention. A Trendyol developer showcased a solution architecture that integrated Kubernetes, Elasticsearch, and OpenTelemetry—a topic right up my alley.

Yet, something kept my excitement from fully taking off, despite the content's merits. The presenting developer seemed to have a problem that no one could help him with at that moment: he was extremely shy. His deeply ingrained shyness made him speak in an excruciatingly quiet voice, and he mumbled constantly. Although the audience remained silent, it didn't help. By the end of the presentation, I had managed, through great effort, to understand enough to make it worthwhile. Still, it was far from a pleasant experience.

That said, situations like this call for understanding. After all, many developers use small, free tech meetups as practice grounds for larger gigs with paying, professional audiences.

The second speaker of the evening delivered his talk in a much clearer and more comfortable tone. Unfortunately, his topic was less technical and felt more like a sales pitch for Elasticsearch products.

Ultimately, I gained the most from the first presentation, despite its challenges.

Berlin is surprisingly full of places that, to a passionate pedestrian like me, seem like islands. Most of the time, however, a quick glance at Google Maps disappoints me by revealing it's just a peninsula or a strangely shaped river. On the evening of Tuesday, July 2, 2024 (#94), I found myself heading to Hallerstraße 6—one of those places.

I have a good habit of arriving much too early for meetings and events. Out of a sense of politeness and not wanting to bother the hosts, I usually spend the extra time taking a stroll through the nearby streets. That evening, tired and drained from a regular workday, I wandered through the neighborhood surrounding the IAV Digital Lab, the actual event venue. For a brief moment, I was convinced I was on an island.

Finally, I thought, I had made it to one of Berlin's legendary islands. But it didn't seem like an ordinary island. A cluster of companies and institutes gave it the atmosphere of a workshop for car enthusiasts—a place that felt like it could be summed up with the phrase: "Plaid shirts and traffic jams, I'm studying mechanical engineering." Of course, readers with worldly, sophisticated humor might replace *traffic jams* with another kind of *jam*. *(Note from the German author: The essence is lost in translation from the original German text.)*

This focus on automobiles made the island feel even more surreal to me. What on earth were car tinkerers doing in Berlin? In my mind, Berlin isn't car country. I could think of dozens of other cities and regions where the "Lightbulb Peninsula" (as ChatGPT referred to a Google Maps screenshot of it) with its car enthusiast workshops would have been a much better fit.

Perhaps—just perhaps—the tinkerers of Germany's old automotive republic were frustrated back then that, despite their wealth and success, the best parties were all happening in Berlin. As a solution, they decided to establish an enclave in the middle of Europe's party capital, Berlin. Naturally, they assured their investors that it was proximity to the Bundestag, not Berghain, they were after.

In the end, everyone was happy, and as a result, a young software architect like me got the chance in 2024 to visit the IAV Digital Lab on Hallerstraße 6.

In the offices of the Ingenieurgesellschaft Auto und Verkehr (IAV), the Automotive Security Research Group (ASRG) once again delivered a phenomenal presentation. During a brief introduction, a representative from IAV recounted the company's modest beginnings as a spin-off of the Technical University of Berlin. But even more captivating was the subsequent introduction by John Heldreth, the founder of ASRG.

He conveyed how the now globally recognized organization, with thousands of members, had essentially originated from his master's thesis. It had scaled far beyond his initial expectations, to the point where it sometimes felt almost overwhelming. I found his story deeply inspiring. Secretly, I hoped that my own "Event Report" project might one day spiral into similar, unanticipated success.

John also used his introduction to highlight a new ASRG product, which I found even more exciting than his already impressive success story. In collaboration with the cybersecurity company VicOne, ASRG had developed a database tailored to the automotive industry for tracking software vulnerabilities, making it publicly accessible.

At exactly 10:56 a.m. on October 19, 2024, I typed "Toyota" into the database's search bar in my browser. The result? Five vulnerabilities, each complete with a CVE identifier. Simply brilliant.

Otherwise, my "lightbulb peninsula evening" focused more on post-quantum cryptography and its integration into vehicle software systems—classic ASRG topics.

After a brief breather in Riga, during which I indulged in an extended visit to the local McDonald's in the city center, I resumed my event tour. In Berlin, all IT event roads don't lead to Rome—they lead to Google's office at Tucholskystraße 2 (#95).

Although I tried not to attend Google events too frequently to maintain variety in my reports, sometimes it was unavoidable—because, on certain evenings, a classic Google event was simply the best option. And on the evening of Wednesday, July 17, 2024, I wasn't disappointed.

Over the course of six technical presentations, I learned so much new information that I quickly forgave myself for my 'Google sin.' I shed my tunnel vision, opened my mind wide, and let a flood of inspiration from the world of software architecture wash over me.

On the agenda were: RAG à la PostgreSQL, function calls within the Gemini language model, vector search scaling with Milvus, Docker's new test containers, massive time-series analyses with InfluxDB, and load testing LLMs with Gatling.

All in all, it was quite an educational evening.

Chapter 20 - Gourmet Bananas

Since kindergarten, I've struggled with my enthusiasm—or more accurately, with the social feedback I receive because of it. I can recall specific moments from kindergarten, school, university, and even my professional life, where my bursts of enthusiasm were met with silence and cautious glances from my peers. These moments were rare and infrequent enough that they didn't stop me from pursuing my projects, but they did make me reflect.

And so, today, on October 22, 2024, I pose this somewhat pop-psychology-inspired question to ChatGPT: "Why does excessive enthusiasm for a topic make other people uncomfortable and cause them to withdraw?" ChatGPT responds with way too much text. The generation immediately following mine (or perhaps a fraction of my own) might say: "Too much yap in Yaptown."

So, I follow up with: "Shorten your response to four concise sentences." ChatGPT reins itself in and provides the following summary:

"Excessive enthusiasm can make others uncomfortable if they don't share the interest or feel inferior as a result. It often creates pressure because the enthusiast unconsciously expects others to mirror their passion. Monologues that disregard the listener's perspective can come across as one-sided and lead to distance. Strong emotions or breaking social norms can further trigger unease."

This makes it sound, at least partly, like it's my fault. Naturally, for my own self-preservation, I'm not willing to let that stand. So, I shift from defense to offense.

So, my next prompt to ChatGPT was: "Tell me why so many people suffer from a lack of enthusiasm." Once again, the California-based AI tried to bury me under a mountain of text. I quickly responded with another prompt: "Less yap, please." ChatGPT understood and replied succinctly:

"Many people lack enthusiasm due to stress, mental health issues like depression, or a monotonous daily routine. Negative experiences, where their enthusiasm was poorly received, can also lead them to suppress it."

This response cut through my combative stance. Instead of remaining on the offensive, I was overcome by a wave of deep empathy for others. It was a rollercoaster of emotions I hadn't anticipated. To help others—and my future self—out of this rut, I continued prompting: "Give me a strategy to counteract a lack of enthusiasm. Keep it brief."

Without overwhelming me with verbosity, the precursor of future superintelligences responded: *"Set small, achievable goals that interest you and celebrate your progress. Regularly introduce new activities or hobbies into your routine to spark fresh inspiration. Reflect on your successes and focus on positive experiences. Avoid burnout by planning breaks and maintaining a balance between rest and activity."*

The response resonated with thoughts already swirling at the edge of my consciousness. Sometimes, my job as an IT consultant felt a bit dull and uninspired. On those days, I'd drag myself, tired and drained, to the next event. Then something almost magical would happen: the people and the presentations at these events would reignite my spirit.

Buoyed and inspired, I'd tackle the next workday with renewed energy—even if, on such mornings, I had less sleep than usual thanks to the evening event.

I set myself small, achievable goals along the way. First, it was the first 10 events, then 20, then 30 that I wanted to attend and document. As I continually fueled my enthusiasm, I steadily approached my larger goal of attending and documenting 100 events. Eventually, there were only five left to reach that milestone.

On Thursday, August 1, 2024, I found myself near Ostbahnhof at an event hosted by the Deutsche Bank Berlin Technology Centre (#96). With a well-measured dose of enthusiasm, I even managed to convince a friend working in the tech sector to join me. Together, we listened intently to two presentations—one about developing robust frontend applications and another about the concept of a "test trophy."

As I was currently working on setting up automated integration testing at my job, the second presentation resonated deeply with me. I was already familiar with the concept of the test pyramid, but the idea of a test trophy was entirely new to me. I absorbed every word of the talk and resolved to incorporate some of the ideas into my daily work.

The evening ended on a doubly positive note when I managed to snag a Tex-Mex pizza with a sausage-stuffed crust at a nearby Netto.

Seven days later, I went alone to the next event, as my enthusiasm for inspiring others to join me in the Berlin offices of JetBrains was, unsurprisingly, not very high (#97). On the other hand, I didn't really make much effort to cultivate that kind of enthusiasm, so it wasn't a significant loss for me.

The event was a meeting of Quality Engineering Berlin, a group I had first encountered five months earlier at the offices of ThoughtWorks, near the Berlin Ostkreuz S-Bahn station (#83). Back then, I had the impression that the speakers favored lighter, more philosophical topics over deep dives into technical enthusiasm.

I deliberately tried to focus my event reports on technology and its applications. My intention wasn't to sift through Berlin's tech scene only to end up writing yet another generic self-help book. At least, not yet. Perhaps one cold, dark winter evening, after a big glass of mulled wine and half a ton of spekulatius cookies, I might be tempted. But even that scenario seemed highly unlikely since, by that point, I hadn't touched alcohol or sweets for several years.

This time, they pulled out all the stops. Two of the three talks that evening at JetBrains were of a more "philosophical" nature. It was, at times, excruciating. Not that I'm opposed to "philosophical" content—it just needs to maintain the right pace. And that pace was completely off.

Content that I'd typically consume in two minutes—like listening to a podcast or reading a book—as if I were some investment banker snorting a line of ruthlessness before an important client meeting, was dragged out over what felt like 60 minutes. Any good dealer, I assume, knows not to dilute their product too much, or they'll lose their paying customers.

Despite the occasional agony of sitting through it, the evening was salvaged by a JetBrains developer. His talk delved into countless technical details, giving me the opportunity to fill my report with substantial, meaningful content after all.

Four days later, I once again climbed the spiral staircase at TMF e.V. on Charlottenstraße 42 to attend the 162nd Health IT Talk (#98). Once again, I felt uneasy in the presence of the regular crowd, which consisted mainly of older white men. I had nothing against older white men—mainly because, God willing, I'll eventually become one myself. Still, they made me feel uncertain.

It started with the question of whether I should address them using *Du* or *Sie* (informal or formal "you"). At one of my usual English-language events, this wouldn't be an issue, since English doesn't differentiate between the two. Technically, it shouldn't have been a problem in German either, if it weren't for the professional context's ambiguous *Du*-culture. At my workplace, for instance, everyone used *Du* without the older person needing to offer it to the younger one first.

The age difference added to my unease. Most of the attendees at the Health IT Talk appeared to be 50+, which meant I was sitting among people 20 to 30 years older than me. At my usual events, the gap was usually half that. Another factor that heightened my insecurity was my lack of expertise in Health IT, which made me hesitant to start conversations for fear of embarrassing myself.

On top of all that, I couldn't shake the feeling that the kind of casual small talk that seems so natural in English might come across as awkward or even irritating in German.

Dozens of reasons and rationalizations came to mind that I could use to justify my minimal interactions with the other participants at the Health IT Talk. But at some point, I knew I just had to give it a try. That evening, I managed a small victory when I struck up a brief, nervous small-talk conversation with my old, white, German-speaking seatmate about the broken air conditioning.

Step by step, I hoped I was inching closer to conquering the "beast" of the old, white, German-speaking man. One day, I imagined, I might tame it and forge an alliance that would enable me to take on real dragons—like the tax office or stingy employers.

Still, the evening wasn't wasted. Two presentations provided us with a wealth of knowledge about the world of digital patient portals, which made it worthwhile.

Exactly one week later, I was back on familiar ground. At *hubraum*, the tech incubator of Deutsche Telekom, Chainlink Berlin hosted an event for Web3 developers and enthusiasts (#99). As is often the case at Web3 meetups, the crowd was a mix of the usual developers and a few sketchy characters.

As expected, these types listed places like Dubai or Malta as their residences and loved to talk about Web3—without delving into the underlying technology. Perhaps they didn't fully understand it themselves, or maybe the technology's actual structure was less impressive than the colorful websites and buzzwords on their company pages suggested.

That evening, I had the opportunity to expand my Web3 vocabulary with the word *oracle*. In the Web3 context, I think the term *reverse oracle* would be much more fitting. Traditionally, an oracle—like the Oracle of Delphi in ancient Greece—was a place or infrastructure connecting the earthly with the spiritual world. The direction of the information flow in the classic sense is clear: a person from the earthly realm seeks prophecy or information from the spiritual realm.

In the modern Web3 context, however, the flow of information is reversed. Elements of the "spiritual world," such as smart contracts, want to access information from the earthly world—like the weather—to make decisions that, in turn, trigger immaterial financial flows.

After my evening crash course in Greek mythology, I was just one event away from reaching my grand goal of attending 100 events.

The following week, however, I took an involuntary but welcome break. An ICE train whisked me away from my concrete-jungle neighborhood to a surprisingly green spot in the Ruhr region. There, I met with my colleagues at the client's office to discuss important IT consulting matters.

The trip was a refreshing change from the monotony of daily home office life. It was also the first time I met some of my colleagues in person. At lunchtime, I had the pleasure of indulging in *frikandellen* at a Dutch snack bar with my favorite client contact—a rare treat.

The decisive evening finally came on September 5, 2024, at the Berlin office of HelloFresh (#100). Between my first event on June 9, 2022, at the DAMA Stammtisch in Hamburg (#1) and my hundredth event (#100), there were roughly two years and three months. I'd be lying if I said I felt anything celebratory on that September evening. It was pure routine.

The topic of the evening—LLMs (large language models) and the vector databases used in that context—fit perfectly with the hype of the moment. As I looked at the large crowd of attendees, I couldn't help but reflect on how many times I had seen only a handful of participants at events covering less trendy topics. A wave of melancholy washed over me, and I found myself mentally withdrawing. Following the well-trodden path of the masses felt dreadfully uninspiring.

On my way home, I debated whether I should celebrate my "great" achievement with a feast. Somehow, I wasn't in the mood, so I settled on a middle ground. I bought a bunch of *gourmet bananas* for one euro at an Edeka. However, unfamiliar with the peculiar texture of gourmet bananas, I only ate half before collapsing into bed, tired and drained.

Epilogue

There he was again, the grinning golden boy. The same mischievous smile on his face as back in high school, when he effortlessly and elegantly shattered my self-esteem during the lower grade reading competition. Back then, he was the universally adored, athletic heartthrob from the neighboring class, and I was the unpopular, chubby outsider. With his reading skills, he wiped the floor with me.

It was a defeat I no longer shed a tear over, but at the time, it hit me hard. After all, my pride and self-worth were entirely tied to my love of reading. I thought no one in my year could hold a candle to me when it came to books. I knew the library in our small town like the back of my hand. During summer vacation, I would read the books for the upcoming school year just for fun.

But instead of dazzling everyone with my book, *The Girl Under the Bridge* by Nina Rauprich, I had to watch, dejected, as the boy who already had everything also took the last shred of my pride from me.

More than 15 years later, my greatest rival and I are now best friends. Today, I feel genuine appreciation and respect for the charismatic golden boy, even though I still haven't entirely shaken my envy of him and his achievements. Watching him earn every single one of his laurels through sheer hard work and sacrifice— something I witnessed firsthand—didn't make it any easier. Where was my success? Where were my laurels?

On one hand, his presence felt like a constant reproach that left me despairing. On the other, it was a persistent call to action, urging me onto better paths.

Sometimes, I felt like Cain, seeing him as Abel. Why were his efforts and sacrifices rewarded more richly than mine? Deep down, I knew the answer. My sacrifices weren't sincere. I gave, but never in a way that truly cost me anything. No sweat, no reward, as the saying goes. But I wanted the reward without shedding the sweat.

That realization terrified me. I never wanted to face the dreadful question: "Am I my best friend's keeper?" Somehow, I had to learn to become more genuine, more honest in my efforts. Whether I would succeed, I didn't know. But I hoped.

It's March 16, 2024. My best friend and I are standing on a ferry chugging across the Wannsee. After we disembark, I shoo away some wild geese on the far side of the shore while my old reading buddy and I talk about big ideas. At a nearby gas station, we grab a eucalyptus gum, which jolts me out of a light drowsiness and back into the world of the awake—a secret tip from my successful lawyer friend, the king of readers.

Leisurely, we make our way back to the ferry. Life is good. The journey is long. The price of eucalyptus gum is acceptable.